Dawns
with
Dexter

Dawns *with* Dexter

RON BALL

**Executive
Books**

Dawns With Dexter

Published by
Executive Books
206 West Allen Street
Mechanicsburg, PA 17055

Copyright © 2005 by Ron Ball

Cover Design and Interior Layout by Gregory A. Dixon

ISBN: 0-937539-94-5

Printed in the United States of America

CONTENTS

INTRODUCTION

I first met Dexter Yager in 1985. At that time I was finishing five years as a special assistant to Dr. Charles Stanley at the First Baptist Church of Atlanta, Georgia. I found out Dexter was enormously successful in what was known at that time as Amway.

The majority of Amway's business around the world was in some way under Dexter. His influence and reach was literally worldwide. He was responsible for sponsoring conventions around the world that attracted hundreds of thousands of people. Millions had heard his messages and read his books.

This is my story of how this world leader decided to mentor a young man who was virtually unknown and had zero business experience. It is a story of how one man chose to pour his life into another.

CHAPTER 1

The First Dawn

When I was a student at Asbury College in Kentucky, I developed a dream for spiritual influence. I had a great hunger for an opportunity to spread a positive message around the world. I would sit sometimes for hours and pray, consider, reflect. What can I do? How can I do it?

Someone gave me a book during my senior year of college about the world renowned figure Billy Graham. I was fascinated as I dug more deeply into that book than any of my regular school text materials. I was interested in finding out everything that I could learn about this great and Godly man. I read about his early experiences. His difficulties and his moments of adversity. I read about his integrity and his whole-hearted commitment to help people spiritually.

The more I read this book, the more I was captured by a desire to do the same thing. I was involved in a number of student outreach programs. I was traveling on the week-ends. I was speaking in churches and at civic groups and different organizations. More and more the desire developed within me to make a world-wide difference for God. And because of that I began to discipline myself in ways that I'd never done before.

In all honesty, I went to college for one basic reason. To meet girls. And my grades reflected that. And my commitments reflected that. But something changed during that senior year of college. A seriousness, a hunger, a desire for something significant exploded within me.

When I finished Asbury College I met and married my wife Amy. She became a dream for me. A dream come true. Her vivacious personality, her physical attractiveness, her spiritual excitement, all began to reach my heart on levels that no other girl ever had. I'd dated over a hundred different girls while I was in college. Remember, I went to meet girls!

Amy, however, was different. We went on our first date in Lexington, Kentucky. I remember driving with Amy on a beautiful June day and Amy began to sing. I had never had a date sing before. This was something entirely new. She began to sing great praise and worship songs about Jesus Christ and her relationship with God. She felt so comfortable and so free with me that I began to try to sing along. Well, I'm terrible! She laughed. And I laughed.

Then we did everything I could think of for the rest of the evening to occupy our time. We went bowling; we played miniature-golf; we went to a local junk food restaurant for hot fudge sundaes. I realized quickly that I was with someone who was not only fun, but also someone who had a spiritual depth that challenged and excited me.

Amy and I were married the next year. I then was accepted as a student in graduate school and worked for three years on a Masters Degree program. I was working, speaking, traveling, newly married. It was an exciting and rich time for both of us.

Then I was encouraged by one of my professors to apply for a doctoral program at Emory University in Atlanta, Georgia. I applied at Emory, as well as two other schools. I was very excited when I received the acceptance letter from Emory. I also applied for a full academic scholarship and received the good news of being accepted into that program as well.

I finished my Master's Degree and Amy finished her undergraduate college degree and we moved to Atlanta. Our first apartment was on Church Street in Decatur, Georgia. We were young and inexperienced, but full of the promise of the future.

When I began my classes I had to select a foreign language. I had taken Greek in college but I needed a more contemporary language, not the ancient Greek of the New Testament. I agreed to take German as my language. I was consumed with the necessity to pass this class. So for the first few months I would go to doctoral classes, take German and barely survive.

During this time I was asked by a local church to become an associate pastor for student outreach. Amy and I were amazed to discover that the metro area of Atlanta had over 70,000 college students in residence. The church invited me to work part-time and do something to present a positive Christian message to as many students as possible.

So here I was, recently married, working in a PhD program at a highly respected, well-known university, and working part-time at a large church, trying to develop an outreach to students that would make a difference to them spiritually. It was a packed and demanding time of my life.

During this experience I had something unusual occur. The church I was in was a good church, but was affiliated with what we would term today as a more liberal denomination. I was beginning to have serious doubts about it's doctrinal positions. My commitment to Christ had only grown and my certainty that the Bible was entirely and absolutely trustworthy had only strengthened. But this church denomination did not agree with my conviction of the inerrancy of the Bible. I could not with good conscious continue to accept my professional relationship with that denomination.

During this time of tremendous turmoil within me I received an invitation to attend a concert at the First Baptist Church of Atlanta. The pastor was Dr. Charles Stanley, whom I'd never met. I had only watched him on television. Dr. Stanley encouraged everyone to come that week to a concert of a group called TRUTH. I had heard some of their recordings and with great excitement I told Amy, "We have to go to this concert."

We made all the arrangements. We were sitting in the balcony of this large downtown Baptist church. The concert was fantastic and the music exciting and full of positive and uplifting melody and content.

But what really reached me was when Charles Stanley stood up and began to pour his heart out and communicate a burning, blazing commitment to Jesus Christ. I looked at Amy and said, "I wish we were a part of this church. This is amazing! This is an atmosphere that is ALIVE with God. It is electric with power." I wanted more of it. So, I began to sneak over on different occasions and slip into the Sunday evening and Wednesday night services of this vibrant, growing Baptist church.

One day Amy and I had a Sunday off. There was nothing scheduled because it was part of my vacation time. We had thought about going back to visit my family in Kentucky. But instead of that, we said, "Why don't we go over and hear Charles Stanley again." So Amy and I went and sat in the balcony.

During Dr. Stanley's vibrant message I was suddenly and wholeheartedly consumed with a desire to speak to him personally. It was more, in fact, than a desire. It was a conviction. Almost a compulsion. I was overwhelmed with the sense that there was some element of destiny involved with this man in my life and I was supposed to speak to him and find out how I could understand what was happening inside my heart at that moment.

At the end of the service I went to the back foyer. I later discovered that Dr. Stanley did not normally go to that part of the church at the end of a service. He usually went to another part of the church and left quickly because of the press of the crowds around him. But that particular day when I walked to the back foyer, there stood Charles Stanley alone.

There were thousands of people in attendance that morning and most of them wanted to speak to him personally. And there he was. Amy and I walked over. I stuck out my hand and said, "Hi, I'm Ron Ball. This is my wife Amy. I am an associate pastor at a church in this city. And I am facing the greatest crisis of my life. Can I see you?"

Dr. Stanley looked at me with great intensity. After a moment he said, "Call my office tomorrow. I'll arrange for something this week. How would Wednesday be?" I thanked him and he gave me a phone number and then we left.

I later found out that Dr. Stanley had been booked up for 6 months for personal appointments. No one had been able to schedule any opportunity with him until the following year. Yet he said for me to come in. I did not know at the time how remarkable that was.

Monday came. I made the call. His secretary was expecting my communication. I went to see him on Wednesday. For 2 ½ hours I told him of my frustration with the particular denomination with which I was connected. I told him of my disappointment with the doctoral program. Not that Emory was not excellent. It was. But there was something else I hungered to do. There was more that I wanted to experience. I had realized that I did not want an academic career. I did not want to be in a teaching position. I did not want an academic degree. I wanted to go out and do something "earth shattering" for God.

So he listened. And I'm sure that years latter he remembers a very young man in his twenties, who expressed himself with immaturity and too much in a hurry. But he treated me with immense respect and told me that God wanted to lead my life.

He referred to an experience in his own life when he was a young man. His grandfather had been a Pentecostal minister. Charles had become very close to him. He had spent time with him; very valuable time. This was a mentor when he had needed one because Charles' own father had died when Dr. Stanley was a baby.

When this grandfather began to mentor and direct him, Charles Stanley was like the proverbial sponge soaking in every available insight and element of knowledge from this loving grandfather. Dr. Stanley told me how the grandfather said, "Charlie, what do you do if God tells you to do something?" And Dr. Stanley said, "Well, Granddad, I... I... I would do it. Wouldn't I? I would do it?"

And his grandfather said, "Well Charlie, yes you would do it. In fact, if God tells you to put your head through that brick wall over there you just head for the wall and you let God do the rest. Because more important than anything else in your life is to always obey God."

At this moment Charles Stanley leaned forward and looked at me, an unknown youth pastor from another denomination whom he had never met prior to that week, and said, "Ron, that's what God is saying to you today. It doesn't matter whether you can calculate the results, or figure out your finances, or create a situation that will make your decision work. No. You just have to know in the depths of your heart and spirit what God wants you to do with your life. Then if God tells you to head for a brick wall, you just head for the wall and you let God do the rest. I want to give you the same message that my grandfather gave me—that obedience to God is more important than anything else in your life."

I was numbed. I had no response. I mumbled a word of thanks and had a prayer and the meeting was over. I walked to my car dazed. I was overwhelmed by the implications of what Dr. Stanley had said. I had a scholarship. I had a job. I was about to get a PhD. I had a teaching position that had already been offered to me. I had a young wife to support. I had every reason to keep on my same career path.

But I knew it was wrong. I knew that God wanted to show me something different. Here was a mentor who gave me what I needed. Not what I wanted. Not what I looked for, but what I needed at a critical moment in my life.

I went back to Kentucky having resigned the scholarship and having withdrawn from the PhD program feeling a lightness and happiness and spring in my step that I had not felt for well over a year and an half. Amy was loyal, committed, supportive, and went with me to Kentucky. I began to try to get speaking engagements. I had none. I had no money. My mother and father were giving me financial support. They were providing rent money and grocery money while I tried to find some employment.

Then a church asked me to speak. Then another. And another. And another. And during that process I knew that God was honoring my decision to move into a faith position.

There is a verse in the book of Hebrews in the Bible. It is a wonderful book dealing with great spiritual insight and development. That verse says, "Without faith it is impossible to please God." So I knew that I had to move into a faith adventure. The fear, the anxiety, the worry, the concern only seemed to exhilarate the two of us more. We were living on the edge of the unknown. But we knew that God was in command of that unknown. So our security was not in our decision making. And our security was not in our ability, or our contacts, or our networking. Our security was in God, Himself, and His direction for the two of us.

It was an interesting year. We lived in a small apartment in Lexington. I went to as many church crusade meetings as possible. We took up offerings. Some weeks we barely had money to survive. There were occasions when Amy and I would sleep in our car at rest stops on interstates because there was no money for a hotel. We would take what little food was given to us at a church dinner and put it in a bag, or box, and we would carefully eat that for two or three days until it was gone.

I remember once we had a few extra dollars and we decided to do something extraordinary. We splurged! We went to a local fast food restaurant called Long John Silvers. We ordered a kids meal. One piece of fish. Small order of fries. One small kid size coke. I looked at the man at the counter and said, "Can we have some extra crumblies please?" And he said, "Of course!" What he didn't know was that those extra crumbliest were the balance of our meal. So he poured them on. Amy and I sat there and there was a happiness and an "alive" quality to everything about our life at that point that made up for the lack of food and material comfort because we had such excitement about where we were going.

We stayed in touch with Dr. Stanley. He gave me his home phone number. Every two months I would call him and give a brief report. He would just say, "Ron now remember, you just continue to trust God. You continue to expect God's support. Because you are trying from you're heart to do what's right.

There were moments of frustrations and disappointments. There were times when things went bad. We managed to generate enough income to hire someone to help us with office and clerical work while we developed some of our Christian outreach opportunities. It turned out to be a disastrous decision. It was someone who took advantage of our money and our resources.

I remember the lowest moment came when I found out that the individual we had hired had not paid the Internal Revenue Service our tax money for that year while we were trying to work with developing this church outreach. I sat on the steps of our apartment and thought, "It's over. It's over. I now have the IRS wanting all this money. It's just over. There's no way that I can ever pay this amount of money. We're so broke. We're so poor. We're so desperate for a means to live. I can't come up with thousands of dollars in penalties and taxes." Yet the Internal Revenue was threatening us severely. We were confused and hurt.

The next day I was walking through our small apartment still with no idea of what to do and simply begging God to help us. Without any warning I had a sudden sense that I should call a women in the small town in Eastern Kentucky where I had grown up. This women had been a friend of my family for a number of years. I didn't know why I was supposed to call her. I knew she was a saintly woman with a tremendous prayer outreach all over the world and a woman of great spiritual integrity and character. But I called her.

And she said, "Well Ron! I haven't heard from you in years. What's going on?"

I just blurted it out. "Phyllis. I don't know what to do. I don't know how to handle this. We have to come up with so much money for the IRS this week."

And she said, "Well how much is it?"

I told her it was so many thousands of dollars. And I told her to the penny and 32 cents. Thousands, thousands, thousands and 32 cents.

And she said, "Ron this is amazing. I have a special tithing and giving account. It's a special account that I give to special Christian causes. And she said, "In that account is a certain amount of money. This week I was going to write a check to a nationally known Christian television ministry. And I just felt in my heart God saying, 'No Phyllis. No. That money is for someone else.'"

So Phyllis said, "Ron I want you to be ready for this. But the amount in that account is exactly the amount you just told me about. Even down to the 32 cents. Where should I send the check?"

I sat down on the floor. I cried. I cry now even remembering it. Because again God had intervened at a critical moment to show us His reality...His character...His love for us. God gave us Charles Stanley as a spiritual mentor and now Phyllis Ranier as a financial mentor. She began to give us counsel on how to organize ourselves and to put together our financial situation.

A few months later I came into the bedroom and said, "Amy, do you know what we're supposed to do next?"

And she said, "No. What are we supposed to do next?"

I said, "We're supposed to move back to Atlanta and go to Charles Stanley's church and grow spiritually even more."

And she said, "Well, then let's go!"

So we packed up and moved to Atlanta and stayed with friends for a few days.

One afternoon we were driving around and a new house was being built. Not a big house. Just a new house. And I thought, "Wouldn't it be incredible to own a house! But we have no money. So I called my friend Phyllis who had been my financial advisor for these few months. I said, "Would you pray for us. We really need to buy a house."

She said, "How much is the down payment?"

I told her and she said, "Isn't it amazing? That's the exact amount that's in my giving account this month. Where shall I send the check?"

So she sent the check. We bought the house. We began to attend the church. I did a few church crusade meetings. I wasn't paid much. I loved speaking. I went and told Charles Stanley I was back in town and was there for the sole purpose of just being mentored; learning; being under his ministry.

For several months everything stayed status quo. Nothing moved. Nothing much happened. Money trickled in. My mother and father continued to give us wonderful help. During that year we found out that Amy was pregnant. 8 months later we gave birth to a premature little girl who only weighted 4 lb 10 oz. We named her Allison Joy. She was healthy. She was just tiny.

During that time a new baby...speaking at a few church meetings....little amounts of money coming in...we began to experience another financial discouragement. While we were trying to develop where we were going and what we were doing, it became so desperate that I went to a junk yard one day and sold the hubcaps off my car to buy milk and diapers and food for little Allison.

During this time a man had helped us buy a small motor home to take to church meetings. We didn't have a car. We even went to the grocery store in this little motor home and had difficulty affording the gas for it. But we would limp from week to week and meeting to meeting.

A friend of ours named Beverly called one day and said, "Ron, we are going to Disney World and we were going to go down in a friend's motor home, but the friend has chicken pox. Will you take us in your motor home? We'll pay your way and pay for gas and pay the hotel and pay for tickets for you to go to Disney World!"

Allison was only 6 months old and we thought, "This will be neat. We'll do it." So we went down. I got strep throat on the trip. Everyone else had a fabulous time and I lay in the trailer miserable, feverish and hoping I could get out and enjoy the beautiful weather. Eventually after two days I recovered sufficiently to join everyone in their fun.

While we were away, a phone message came into our answering

machine at our house in Marietta, Georgia. I didn't know the message had come. All the time we were in Disney World for four days, that little message unit beeped and beeped and beeped with that one message.

We got home 4 ½ days later and walked into the house and there was the machine...beep, beep, beep waiting for us. I pushed the button. There was a message from a staff member at the First Baptist Church Atlanta.

He said, "Dr. Stanley would like to know if you would speak for him next Sunday night. Please call us immediately."

I thought, "Oh no! I've been gone four days. I quickly tracked this man down and I said, "I'll do it! I'll do it!"

He said, "Well, we thought you might be away and we were getting ready to make some other arrangements. But you've called in time and we'd be glad to have you next Sunday night."

I went. Very scared. Very nervous. Squeaky voice. Not knowing what to do. I spoke that night. People were wonderful. A couple of thousand people in the crowd. It was a nerve racking, but wonderful experience.

A few months later Dr. Stanley called personally and asked, "Ron, could you do all the services next Sunday? Sunday morning. All of them. And Sunday night. The whole day?"

And I said, "Yes sir. I'll be happy to."

So I spoke at all the services that next Sunday. And then he asked me to speak another Sunday. And another. And yet another. He was busy during this time working with the Southern Baptist Convention. There was a movement and a ground swell of commitment to elect him the president. To my knowledge he never sought it. It was a time of great challenge in the denomination when liberal and conservative forces clashed for the leadership of this historic denominational group. So he was away a lot and he asked me to frequently speak.

One Wednesday night I was at the church just to hear him. I wasn't speaking. He was walking down the hall alone, which again was rare. It almost never happened.

He stopped and said, "Ron, I've been wanting to talk to you. Would you be willing to assist me? To be my preaching assistant? To speak for me while I'm away. I don't know how long it will take. I don't know what it will involve. But we will work around your other speaking commitments and obligations." I was still speaking in different churches. But he said, "We will make it work. Will you do it?"

So for the next 4 ½ years, that's what I did.

During that time of mentoring; during that time of growth; during that time of spiritual education; my walk with God began to deepen; my commitment to the Bible was strengthened. I spoke numerous times to the church. I became a part of a church organization, part of the church community. Allison was older, four or five years of age and great things were happening.

During this time I began to feel a frustration that I had not felt during the whole five years. Because when I would be out speaking in different churches, I began to observe that the people I wanted to reach and the people I wanted to tell about how fantastic Jesus Christ is...those people were not coming. I was speaking almost exclusively to church members and church attendees. I wanted to reach the business community, and the movers and shakers of different cities and towns. I wanted to do something to get through to them. But they weren't coming.

One day I went in to see Dr. Stanley and poured out my frustration to him. I said, "What am I going to do?"

Dr. Stanley said, "We need to pray right now that God will open a door for you that will not be conventional. Because I want you to know that conventional evangelism and large crusades are not working the way they used too. They are effective for Billy Graham.

"But generally things are not happening the way they need to or moving the way they could move. We are not reaching the people we need to reach. We're just not. I'm going to pray for God to open something different for you." And he put his arm around me and we prayed and I left.

I went downstairs and sat in my car on a hot June Atlanta day. Sweltering humidity; intense heat. I didn't even turn the car on. I didn't even bother with the air conditioning. I was too affected by what we had discussed. I began to cry. I don't cry easily. I don't cry often. But I cried that day. And I said, "Oh God, show me how to do this."

That year I received an invitation to do a special Holy Week seminar services for the Southern Bell Company and their management. They asked me to come back twice more. And I thought, "This is wonderful. I love speaking to business people. Could this be what I'm supposed to do?" But there was no indication, other than the Southern Bell opportunity, that anything was going to happen.

Charles Stanley continued to pray for me. I continued to work with the church. I filled in for him in meetings where I would meet with dignitaries like Vice President George Bush and others who would come to the city of Atlanta. I would represent Charles Stanley and the church. I had a fantastic time learning and growing and observing him, watching how he worked with people, and having him train me and teach me.

During that time I received an invitation from the church to conduct the annual Marriage Retreat. Now this was an annual event in Hilton Head Island, South Carolina. I was going to speak for a week. There were over a thousand people there; five-hundred couples. I had a great time. I loved every minute of it!

After one of the sessions, a couple came up to me and introduced themselves as Terry and Sandy Thoms. They said they had loved what I said and would love to hear more of it.

Sandy said to me, "There was something in particular that you said that reached my heart. You said, 'I never want to settle for a mediocre marriage. I am willing to work; I'm willing to raise my level of commitment; I'm willing to study; I'm willing to do whatever is necessary so that I will have an extraordinary marriage my whole life and never be mediocre.'" And she said, "I want that too. My husband and I want that. And we want to thank you for that. Can we keep in touch?"

We exchanged phone numbers and I forgot about it.

A couple months later I was doing a church crusade meeting in the small community of Eaton, Colorado. All the churches had come together and I was speaking in a large school auditorium for the week. One afternoon I received a telephone message marked "Urgent" from a Mr. Terry Thoms in Atlanta. I called him back.

He said, "Ron, I have a business. I have someone in my business organization who is having a severe marital challenge. Will you speak to them and give them marriage counseling?"

I apologized to Terry and said, "I'm afraid I cannot do it. There's no way. I do not have the time. You need to find someone else. I wish I could, but I'm just not available."

Terry called the next day with the same message and I gave him the same reply. Terry called the third day again with the same message and I began to get irritated. "Why are you bugging me? Why are you pushing me? I don't have time to do this."

He asked, "Could you just talk to them once? We'll take you and Amy out to dinner if you'll just talk to them once."

At this point, even though I was mildly irritated, I did grudgingly respect Terry's persistence. Also, I began to have a high regard for his positive attitude. I loved it! So I agreed to see the couple. For about a month, I counseled the couple and then at the end of that month I transferred them to someone else.

Terry then said, "Now, I owe you a dinner." So they took us to at that time the tallest hotel in the world, The Peachtree Plaza in downtown Atlanta. Amy and I met Terry and Sandy there and they treated us to a fabulous steak dinner in a revolving restaurant that gradually made a sweep of the entire Atlanta metro and the surrounding areas.

During the conversation at dinner, Terry leaned forward and asked, "Ron, could I introduce you to my hero?" I loved the word "hero" and I knew what it meant, but I was intrigued. It was not a term that you normally heard; at least in modern vernacular.

So I said, "Okay Terry, who is your hero?"

He said, " Well it's my cousin and I want you to meet him."

So I said, "Well great, let's meet him!"

So the next week, we met at the Atlanta Marriot Hotel. His cousin spent about two hours with me. I remember he leaned forward and said, "Ron, what do you believe about success as a Christian?" I answered about how God wants to bless us and we need to work hard and that God wants to give us greater opportunities. I shared how I learned all that from Charles Stanley. I explained Charles is a man of enormous vision and challenge with an exciting work ethic.

So Billy, the cousin, came to my home a week later with some other friends, along with Terry and Sandy and Billy's wife Peggy. They began to quiz me about what I did. At one point Terry said, "Billy, why don't you have Ron speak at your next convention?"

Billy glared at him and I found out later that Billy had a policy that he never asked anyone to speak unless he'd heard them at least on tape. Billy looked back at me and asked, "Well Ron, how many times have you spoken for Charles Stanley these last few months?"

I said, "I don't know. Fifteen, or twenty times."

Billy looked at me and said, "Well, would you like to speak at my spring convention?"

I said, "Sure. I'll do it."

So I went to Gainesville, Georgia and spoke to a wonderful group of success oriented Christians. I didn't even know these phenomenal people existed! They were so excited about life.

All that week-end everyone buzzed about someone I'd never heard of. The other speakers, Jerry and Cherry Meadows, also spoke frequently about this mysterious individual. I was intrigued because every speaker would so elevate this man's wisdom. I thought, "Well, I want wisdom. I want knowledge. I want insight. I want success. I want to serve God. I don't want to waste my time. I want to meet this man." They said his name was Dexter Yager and his wife was Birdie Yager.

I filed it away in my mind and thought I wanted to meet them someday because everyone had so edified them all week-end.

Everyone would tell stories of how something Dexter had said, or something Birdie his wife had mentioned, had changed their life or their income or their direction. I thought I have to meet this amazing person; this mystery figure. So I prayed, "God, in some way, some how, help me meet this man and his wife."

A few weeks later I was traveling with Charles Stanley. We'd been doing meetings in Birmingham, Alabama, and Nashville, Tennessee. We'd been flying to different cities for rallies and just had finished the one in Nashville and driven back to Bowling Green, Kentucky.

We arrived at two o'clock in the morning at the Holiday Inn where we were staying and my phone message light was blinking. I called the operator and she said the message was from a Mr. Jerry Meadows in Franklin, Tennessee. He had said for me to call him at home.

I asked her to wait for a moment while I wrote the number down but thought, "There's no way I can call him tonight because it's 2 o'clock in the morning." So I thanked her and started to hang up but she said, "Well excuse me Mr. Ball, but you have a second message from Mr. Meadows. It reads, 'If you think it's too late to call when you get in...it's not. Please call anyway.'"

I thought, "Two o'clock in the morning...that's what Jerry said." So I called him at home.

He said, "Ron! I'm having a family reunion this summer and it's going to be in Huntsville, Alabama. Would you come and speak for us?"

I thought ,"Why would he want me with his family?" I didn't realize this was a term used in his business for a gathering of all the individuals who were in his multi-level downline. They all gathered together in one place in the summer for what they called a "Family Reunion." I thought it was the Meadows Family. I was ignorant of multi-level businesses at this point.

He said, "The other speakers will be Dexter and Birdie Yager! I'd love for you to meet them."

BINGO! My prayer had been answered. I said, "Hey Jerry, I will be there."

That June, Amy and I went to Huntsville, Alabama. I spoke on Saturday night and also at a special Sunday morning service to present Jesus Christ to people who didn't know Him.

This was a voluntary service and I was thrilled to speak. They also asked me to speak to a leadership group in the afternoon.

I was speaking to the leadership group and the back door opened and in walked Dexter Yager. He'd been speaking that week-end, but I had not met him. He walked in, sat down and listened to me for the next forty-five minutes.

Later Dexter explained to me what had happened. He'd been up all night counseling and mentoring and teaching people and he'd gone to bed at seven in the morning. This was the first indication that I would have that being mentored by a giant like Dexter would involve seeing a lot of sunrises and a lot of dawns. A lot of dawns with Dexter!

He said he'd awakened about an hour before and it was as if God had spoken to him, like an arrow to his heart and said, "Dexter wake up! Get up, right now! Go upstairs. There's someone you're supposed to hear and you're supposed to meet."

Then Dexter next said, "It was you!"

We had a wonderful afternoon together. He was very loving and generous with his time. He and his wife Birdie were exceedingly kind to Amy and me. We had dinner with them and Jerry and Cherry

Meadows. It was a time that I was almost breathless with excitement. I could hardly believe that this was really happening. You would not have expected that Dexter, who was so well known and influential around the world to be so down to earth and easy to talk to and comfortable to be with.

Dexter spent most of his time asking questions of us. He would respond occasionally and say something, that I have to admit...was pretty remarkable! But mostly he just let us talk and was very generous to us individually and as a couple.

The meeting ended and Amy and I went back home to Atlanta. We didn't think much more about it until a few weeks later when I received an invitation to come to Charlotte, North Carolina, to attend one of Dexter's large events. He called it a celebration of Free Enterprise. Well, I thought, "This is really wonderful and I want to go!"

So I went and there were thousands of people at the Charlotte Coliseum. There was an excitement that I'd never seen before. There was a spiritual presence and power that I had not even experienced in church.

There was a presence of Christ, through the Holy Spirit, that was more real than anything that I had ever encountered in my life. On Sunday they had a great Sunday service. Thousands of people attended and hundreds, upon hundreds streamed forward, like in a Billy Graham Crusade, to make public commitments to Jesus Christ as Lord and Savior.

I thought, "Who is this man? Who is this Dexter Yager? This is amazing."

At the end of the Sunday session Dexter invited Amy and me to his lake house. He was building a lake house on Lake Wiley in South Carolina.

He showed us the construction and gave us a tour. We just had a great time. It was absolutely wonderful.

Then Dexter said, "Ron, I'm supposed to help you with something. Did you know that?"

And I thought, "Who am I? I'm nobody. Why would Dexter Yager want to help me?"

But he said again, "I'm supposed to help you. Here is my private, home telephone number. Don't call me before midnight. Only call after midnight."

I called to ask him if he would speak. But before I could dial the number it was as if God stopped me cold and said, "Dexter, do not make this call. Do not schedule a speaker because I'm sending you a speaker."

Dexter looked at me. This was on Saturday night and the Sunday service was the next morning. Dexter said, "Ron, you're that speaker."

I said, "Are you sure?"

He said, "I am totally sure that you're that speaker."

So I rolled out of bed early the next morning at 5:30. I couldn't sleep. I wasn't scheduled to be at the Coliseum until 10 o'clock, but I just couldn't sleep.

I got up. I remember walking in the parking lot of this Marriott Hotel off Tyvola Road in Charlotte, North Carolina. I walked around the cars and the trees and the parking signs. I walked for 2 hours praying. I said, "Lord, you are going to have to help me because there are going to be thousands of people there and a lot of them are business people and I don't know what to say."

It's as if God's spirit said to me, "Well haven't you prayed for this? Haven't you wanted this? What's wrong with you Ron? What's the matter? Isn't this what you've wanted?"

I went to the service. I had trouble starting. I usually don't, but I did that day. But then something happened and God's Spirit took over and I just began to sail through the morning. We had a huge response. It was wonderful.

Dexter had me come back to the lake house that day and he said, "Ron, we need to have a relationship. I have been looking for someone, a pastor, a spiritual leader, who I can teach principles that I know. I'd like you to come over to the house tonight."

I arranged for Amy to spend the time with Birdie his wife. I went over and that night became my first dawn with Dexter. I was exhausted. I was not accustomed to staying up that late. Finally when the sun came up over the lake at 7:00 in the morning I was swaying back and forth, but I wouldn't have missed it for anything.

This man, who had repeatedly said, "How can I help you?" was giving me wisdom and insight beyond what I ever expected. He was telling me straight forwardly, with no embellishment, exactly what I needed to hear. I learned that night and that morning that I was with a man who would tell me the truth. Who would give it to me "between the eyes" as they say. Who would hold back nothing. Who would even hurt me if I needed it. But if I was willing to be mentored then he was willing to do the job.

Sometime after that first dawn with Dexter, Amy and I were in a crunch and I called Dexter. And he said, "Alright, tell me your whole financial situation. I met with him and went through every detail. He said, "You're spending too much money! You're spending money on stupid things...on foolish things." He'd already warned me that he was going to be blunt. He said, "Your eating out alone is destroying your finances. You're going to fancy restaurants and then you're hungry the next day, but your money is gone. You're selfish and self-indulgent and undisciplined."

I was shocked. I said, "Dexter, I thought you said you just loved me and wanted to help me." He smiled this huge grin, with his bearded face and said, "That's exactly what I am doing Ron. I am loving you. I am helping you."

I left that meeting offended. I thought, "I'm not calling Dexter anymore." I didn't want to see him. Really the truth was I didn't want anyone telling me what to do; what to buy; what not to buy. I was selfish. I was self-indulgent. I was self-centered. But I was also broke. I was getting broker. So I humbled myself and called Dexter back and told him I did need his help.

He said, "Why did you call me tonight?"

I told him the truth. I called him at midnight and I told him the truth. I said, "I was praying Dexter. And I said, "God you gotta send me some help. You gotta send me some money. You gotta help me." And a still, small, voice in my heart said, 'Dexter Yager.' I knew I had to call you back."

And I said, "Dex, by the way, I've never asked you this, why do you always have me call you at midnight and the only time I've been with you we stay up to dawn?

He said, "Ron, I'll tell you what. I've learned two things. You make a living from 9-5, but you can find a life from 5 o'clock that other people don't find because they are at their job, or you're at your responsibility. But there is something about the pursuit of quality and the quest and hunger for knowledge. If it will motivate and drive you after you get off work, you're something special. You're not part of a crowd. You're going to stand out.

"The second thing I found out is that speaking to people after work was a good time for them to be available to me to talk about multi-level marketing and direct sales. I was keyed up and I'd stay up. But I found in those early morning hours I would begin to see things I'd never seen before. It did begin to reverse my sleep schedule. That was not my original intention. But that just happened.

"Now I wouldn't trade those nights for anything. In the quiet and stillness of the night, God touches my heart and I think at a depth that I don't often think at during the business of the day. Stick with me Ron. We'll have some great nights and some great dawns! And you'll learn a lot."

So I hung up and a few nights later he had counseled me to sell my house in Georgia. He said, "You need to sell your house. You can't afford it." I didn't want to hear that. I didn't want to sell my house. But I did sell it a few weeks later. I paid off all my debts.

I didn't have any money and I moved back to a little town I grew up in with my parents. Here I was with my wife and my baby daughter living in this back bedroom of my parent's home for months. During that time Amy and I found another house in Georgia. We still didn't have any money, but I had arranged for a bank to give me 100 percent financing.

I called Dexter that night at midnight and said, "Dex, I've found a house. I know that it's only been a few months after I sold the other one. They'll give me 100 percent financing. I know it's a high interest rate. But they said they'll do it. I want to buy this house!"

Dexter, very quietly said, "Ron, I don't think you should. I'm glad to help you. I want to help you. But my counsel is don't buy this house."

I looked at Amy and said, "Dexter says not to buy it. I'll call you back."

He said, "Alright!"

So I prayed. Talked to Amy. Called him back, after midnight, and said, "I'm not going to buy the house."

He said, "Good decision. Why don't you come and see me in a couple weeks. Is it a date? Can you come?"

I said ,"Yes."

He said, "Come late. We're going to stay up. We're going to have another dawn together and I'm going to show you what you can learn by the time the sun comes up when you come and see me again."

When I got there, he told me something that absolutely shocked me. He said, "Ron, I decided that if you had called me back that night and had told me you were buying that house at high interest for 100 percent financing after you had just begun to get out of debt...I would have never worked with you again.

"But I didn't tell you that because I wanted to see the truth. I wanted to see your heart. I wanted to see your character. I wanted to see what you would actually choose to do. I would have never worked with you again."

I was stunned. I said, "Well Dexter, that's amazing." I realized that I had just dodged a bullet and that I was on the edge and had almost fallen over. And he was right. I would have been giving in to my selfishness and my self indulgence and my immaturity and my impulsiveness. But I didn't do it.

There began a mentoring adventure that changed everything about me. There was so much more that I learned from Dexter. That was only the beginning. But I learned that when he said "Ron, I want to help you" that he meant it...and he said it with all of his heart.

CHAPTER 2

Peeling The Onion

I was intrigued by Dexter's personality; his style; his approach. I had never met anyone quite like him. He spoke with insight and warmth and intelligence, but there was a different quality; a different dimension. There was something that I wanted to capture in my own life. One thing that I would continually do when I prayed was to ask God to help me understand this man's thinking. I recognized his extraordinary success; his unusual level of financial and personal achievement. I knew that he exercised influence around the world. I was pleased to have access to someone who had such experience and understanding of national and international events. But there was something more, and I wanted it.

The something more was a quality—an intangible. When I say intangible I don't mean something mysterious or spiritually strange. I mean there was a quality of vision of commitment that I recognized as rare. His focus was legendary. His ability to stay on target toward a goal was beyond anyone I had ever encountered. But he was not harsh. He was not demanding. He was not dominating, or domineering. He was very loving and kind and thoughtful. I knew as I studied him that this was an unusual combination. Here was a man who had tremendous focus and extraordinary commitment, but at the same time had gentleness and sensitivity. This was a combination that I didn't often encounter with high achieving people. My friends in the past that had mentored me had always had these qualities and I was looking for these same qualities in the business world and I soon discovered I had found it in Dexter Yager.

The second time I went to spend a night with him was on a hot summer day. He told me to arrive no earlier than 1:00 p.m. and no later than 2:00 p.m. I did exactly as he outlined and got there between those hours. When I arrived at the house his wife Birdie greeted me and told me to be comfortable and read or relax for a moment because Dexter was still asleep and would be up soon. I was still learning his schedule and his commitment to be "up with the dawn"... meaning that he had not gone to bed the night before. So Birdie said, "Why don't you wait in his office."

Dexter had been building a new house on Lake Wylie in South Carolina. The house was just finished and I was eager to see the result of his dream. Birdie told me they were going to build even a bigger house. She called it the "Log Cabin." This log cabin turned out to have 16,000 square feet and was another dream that Dexter was in the process of accomplishing. But for the time being he was living in a beautiful lake house while he built the "Log Cabin."

I was ushered into his office where eagles abounded! There were eagles on the floor and eagles on the ceiling. Not live birds, of course, but representations of eagles. I learned that the eagle was Dexter's favorite symbol of strength and independence and courage. The eagle motif surrounded me. There was a large window with an eagle imbedded in the glass. There was a desk with porcelain and wood carved eagles. There was a rug with an eagle woven into the fabric. Rather than being overwhelmed by the eagles, I was inspired. I knew that this was a man who loved symbolism. He was motivated by being surrounded by those symbols that reminded him of greatness. He would swim in a continual sea of these reminders. I began to be excited because I thought, "I need symbols in my own life to remind me of the desire to be greater than I am." I realized that if Dexter, a man of such high accomplishment needed these symbols then symbolism would work for me as well.

After about 30 minutes Dexter came in. He was not formally dressed. In fact, he was hardly dressed at all! He had on an undershirt and a pair of gym shorts and an old pair of shoes. He came in a gave me a big bear hug and said, "Ron I'm so glad you could be with me today. There is so much I want to show you and do together with you today."

I thought again how this was a man who had impressed me with his visions and his accomplishments, and yet he was so down to earth and easy to be with and so simple in his relationship approach. He made me feel wonderfully at ease.

We sat for a few minutes and he said, "Now tell me everything that is happening with you."

I realize now that he was beginning a process the way he always did. I did not know it at the time, so I'm going to jump ahead of the story to tell you his methodology. I learned it later, but I'm going to explain it to you now.

He believes that a relationship resembles an onion with layers. He recognizes that these layers would have to be peeled back one after the other until you arrive at a deeper level of relationship understanding. So when he sat down with me on every occasion that I spent with him, he would peel back layers.

"Ron, how are you doing?"

"What's happening with you?"

"Who have you seen lately?"

"What books have you read?"

"What problems have you encountered?"

"What new ideas have excited you?"

He would start this line of conversation and peel back a layer for about an hour. His purpose, I later discovered, was to continue pulling back layers through the course of the day and into the night until we reached the dawn. He believed that in those early morning hours, when the world was quiet and asleep around us, he could peel back even more layers to arrive at a relationship connection with me, or whoever he was with, that would reach depths that an ordinary, conventional conversation would never approach.

That day I answered his questions and we would talk. I still didn't know him that well and I was intimidated because of his influence and his wealth. But at the same time here was a man opening his heart and soul to me and I was hungry for everything that he knew and everything that he could teach me.

I remember that second day. It was a beautiful afternoon and the water surrounded us on three sides. The lake was very large around the point where his house was located and where he was building the log cabin. I would sometimes be captured by the beauty of his environment.

That second day I asked him, "Why are we here? Why are we on the water? What is the reason for this?"

He said, "Well, you know Ron I've always loved water. I realized years ago that the wealthiest, most successful people in the world eventually lived on water. Maybe not full time. Maybe not all the time. But they would live on water at some point."

He went on to say, "Water is an ever changing scene. There is always something interesting and captivating about water. There is always variety and I love that sense of change and the power of the natural world that God created. I find a water environment to be simulating and exciting. I love being on water and so I chose years ago to live on this lake."

I said, "Well Dexter, why did you not choose to live on the ocean?"

Here is where Dexter began to exhibit his practicality. He explained to me why he had picked a lake over the ocean. His reasoning was detailed and specific.

"Well," he said, "an ocean is beautiful and also ever changing and stimulating, as is a lake. Maybe even more so. But it is the "more so" that concerns me. Because the ocean is subject to storms of a level of violence that the lake never sees. Because of that, there's always a certain risk, or danger with the ocean. Ah, I love it! It's stimulating. It's exciting. But it's the excitement that concerns me. Because the excitement of an ocean can reach a level of danger so fast. I thought, well, if I want water but I don't want the potential risk of ocean storms and damage. And I don't want the responsibility of repair and maintenance of a property that is continually exposed to salt air and winds and damaging waves. What is my alternative?"

And he looked at me and smiled and said, "My alternative is the lake! The lake can give me all the pleasure and all the enjoyment that I would get from the ocean...without the liabilities."

I began to realize that this was an unusual man who thought through the details of everything. Here was a man who even calculated carefully what type of water to live on.

So then I said, "Well, tell me more."

He described his search for a water home and how he had found a small piece of property on the water. "Waterfront," he said. "It has to be waterfront."

His property had a small house and he described how he and Birdie had experienced a dramatic comedown to live in that house, but it would be on the water. They moved there and his plan was to tear down the little house and build something more.

Eventually he kept that house and used it as an investment and built somewhere else. But his reasoning is very revealing of his personality and his nature.

He said, "I wanted water and I was willing to live in a smaller house; much smaller than what we're in at that time just to have the peace and tranquility and the enjoyment of the water."

He described to me how when he first walked on that piece of property with the small house he said, "I made a decision."

Now as we go through this book about Dexter you will hear this phrase again...and again: "I made a decision." That is characteristic of him. He makes decisions. He determines by his own choice what he's going to do and when and how he's going to do it.

So when he said, "I made a decision," I listened.

He said, "It's very simple. I made a decision when I walked onto that piece of property. I decided that I would not allow myself to see the small house. I would not permit myself to think in terms of this house being a comedown, or a lower level of living. Instead I would see the water. I would see the wonderful natural beauty of the location. I would always step onto that property with my focus on the water and not on the small and limited house that we would be living in temporarily. Also, I made another decision. I decided it would be temporary."

And he looked at me and said, "Ron, you can put up with a lot if you know it is temporary. If you know it's a stepping stone to something else. If you know it will take you where you want to go."

Then he began to teach me that day about what he called long term thinking. He said, "I am the Long Ranger." He smiled and he said, "That means I always try to see things in the longest term. I always try to see things in a way that will enable me to get to my ultimate goal. So I'm the Long Ranger. I am convinced that one of the challenges with this generation of young men and young women is their relative inability to see long term. They do not understand the principle of delayed gratification. They do not understand that you delay your desires. You delay your gratification. And that you delay your own selfish interests. You delay all that for a greater, grander goal. You delay all that to get something bigger and better."

"So that's why," he said, "I apply that lesson to everything because it gets me to my goals in a happier and faster way. That's what I did when I bought my first property on the lake. It was not going to be my last property. I knew that. So I could put up with the small house. I could put up with the limited living circumstances. I could live with that because there was going to be so much more for me and for Birdie and for my children."

Dexter has seven children. When he says something about the children he is talking about a load of kids! They are all grown now. They have created their own successes and their own lives and careers. Some of them are close friends of Amy and me. When Dexter mentions his kids he always does it with pride and a special sense of commitment. There is a gleam, a glitter in his eye when he speaks of his kids.

He and Birdie started with twins—Dex Jr. and Doyle. Doyle still works with his dad's business enterprises and Dex Jr. has a career of his own. These are the twins, the first born. On down the list there are all the girls and all the boys. There is April, LeAnn, Lisa, Jeff and then the youngest, Steve.

All these kids are an important part of Dexter and Birdie's dream. When Dexter spoke to me of living on the lake he would always mention Birdie and the kids. He loves his wife. He is devoted to her. I have never seen a man more committed to his wife. He sees his children as an extension of himself. They are a special expression of his commitment to Birdie and his love for her.

The Bible's Jewish Old Testament book of Psalms speaks of a man having a quiver full of arrows with the arrows representing children. The Bible connects those children to blessing as a gift of God. So whenever Dexter spoke in the early days of buying property and building his business, he would speak in terms of his children and in terms of his legacy and all that he wanted to create for his wife and his children. He certainly understood what the Bible teaches in that passage.

Dexter spent many years developing his multi-level business. He explained to me that when he would be gone he would arrange his schedule so he would be away for 2 weeks and then he would be home for 2 weeks.

He said, "Ron, during the 2 weeks that I was home, I arranged my life and schedule so that I would be with Birdie and the children more than most people were with their kids and their wife for a whole month! I would be so focused on them. I would concentrate on them for those 2 weeks.

So, 2 weeks away. 2 weeks at home. He had organized this. Then he looked at me and smiled and said, "You know, I made a decision." Now remember that phrase. He said, "I made a decision that my business needed my attention, or it would never grow. But, my wife and my children needed my attention, or they would not grow. So I tried to do both. I know I didn't always succeed. I know there were times when I should have been home more. But I did try to balance building my business and building my family." And he said, "That balance means a great deal to me and still does."

I had brought a notebook and was taking notes. I was eagerly recording everything that he said. I didn't want to miss anything that he wanted to communicate with me on any subject that he could bring up. I wanted it all.

We sat and talked for about 3 hours. The time flew by. Dexter was doing his "onion approach" with me. I didn't realize it at the time, but I do now. He was peeling back layers; asking me questions; digging deeper; offering me insight into his own life and gradually bringing me to a place of trust and relaxation where I would open my heart and soul to this man I was just beginning to know and trust.

Later that evening we jumped in his car and Dex and Birdie and I went out to eat. I was very unacquainted at that point in my life with luxury automobiles. Dexter had a number of cars. Rolls Royce. Mercedes. Jaguar. Old antique cars that he had a special love for. So we picked a Mercedes and went to eat. Dexter had a particular place he wanted to go. I remember it was a buffet with country food and only cost about $4 a piece.

Dexter said, "You know Ron, you don't want to use up all your capital money eating. If you eat out at the wrong place you will spend a great deal of money and a great deal of time and you'll get neither back. So I try to go to a place where the food is well cooked and where there are vegetables and there is a good variety of nutritious food. I try to go to a place that doesn't cost much money."

Years later I heard Dexter telling an interesting story about going into a place and sitting down with a friend to eat. That friend ordered a very expensive item and spent a lot of money on his meal. Then the friend asked Dexter for financial counseling on how to get more money and straighten out his finances.

Dexter said, "I knew that I didn't want to tell the young man that at this point in his life he was self indulgent. He was not a long term thinker. He was not a long ranger. He was spending large amounts of money on food."

Dexter told the story and looked at me and smiled. Then he said, "You know Ron, it's so funny. You know when you eat, you're going to be hungry again the next day. If you eat a $10 meal, you're going to be just as hungry the next day as if you had eaten a $100 meal. So which would you rather do? Find some good food that is less money, or would you rather just spend the money and then be hungry the next day?"

Then I said, "Well what about special occasions? What about a special event?"

He smiled and then said, "Ron, I'm not unreasonable. Of course there are special occasions. Of course there are special events and times that you go out and do something because it is meaningful for someone. Maybe your wife, or someone else. But I'm talking about a general rule of life. A pattern."

I was later to learn that patterns and right habits of success were vital to Dexter. He built his whole life on certain patterns that he would carefully think through, adopt, and then not question. Because that would take care of that part of his life and he had already thought it through. And when it came to food, this was one of those patterns.

He said, "So let's enjoy this meal!"

So for around $4 a person we ate at this country cooking buffet with green beans, mustard greens, kale and corn and tomatoes, lettuce and all kinds of vegetables. I have to admit the food was excellent.

I said, "Dexter, how did you find a place with a meal this good for so little money?"

He said, "Ron I made a decision." Here we go again! "I made a decision that I would do some personal research and find the best place to eat for the money. So I went to a number of restaurants. I took 4 or 5 days and I drove around and I sampled different places and asked local people. Then I found what I was looking for. I found this place and 2 or 3 others so I would have a back up and so I wouldn't tire of one or the other. I decided that here was where I would eat at this point in my life.

I began to gradually understand that this man was one who carefully calculated how he could gain the greatest benefit from his life. How he could gain the greatest benefit from his business. Even his eating and meals mattered to him in helping him accomplish his greater goals.

Now do you think, by what you have already heard, that Dexter Yager is a man who is rigid and difficult to work with? A man who is legalistic and lives by hard rules that he will not break? A man who judges and condemns you if you do not follow those rules? One who judges and condemns himself if he does not follow those rules?

Well, that's not Dexter at all! Here was a man who laughed constantly. He enjoyed everything that he did. What he explained to me was very simple. For example, he would think, "What is the best way to eat for the money?" He figured that out and did it. Here is a man who would think, "How do I get a property on the lake? Well, here's a piece of property on the water. I can afford it, but it has a small house. That's alright. It's on the water. I will chose to enjoy it because it's on the water."

Here is a man who controlled his emotions. Not in a harsh, or hard, or mechanical way. He is not some strange, unfeeling, emotionless robot of a man. No. He is full of life and vitality, and warmth and energy, and excitement and vision. He is a man who uses his God given intellect, to measure and calculate how to reach his goals. He doesn't spend great amounts of emotions arguing with himself or debating or second guessing himself. He just formulates the best, most practical plan, and does it. That frees his energy and time to do greater things.

Dexter would always be trying to stretch me—to enlarge my vision. His whole purpose of eating at a place that released more money was because he knew most people need more money. Here was a simple way to still eat out, but to have more money. If you knew how to control your expenses while eating out it would give you more money to build your business—to build your dream—to build your future. He knew that. He also knew how easy it is to eat out and to spend money without any thought...especially if you make a lot of money and waste more than you realize.

I remember Dexter once jokingly told me how he used to eat out and spend too much money. People would go out with him and he would always announce to the group of friends, "Well, I'll pay!" Then he said, "They would order the most expensive things on the menu and the whole night would cost me hundreds of dollars."

He said, "I don't do that anymore. I learned my lesson. I never tell anybody I'm going to pay until the very end, so they never know. Consistently when I announced that I was going to pay in the beginning everyone would order the most expensive things on the menu. Everybody did!"

He said, "Now I'm not mad at them. I don't feel bad at them. I think it's human nature to grasp an opportunity like that and go for it. But I realized I was teaching my friends the wrong principles about money."

That's another thing about Dexter. He is always teaching. He is always communicating. He is always developing you and helping you to become a better person who can accomplish more in life for God. He is compelled by this. "How do I make you better so that you can serve God and serve your family and serve your fellow human beings more effectively and more productively?" So even all of this was related to eating out that evening.

It was a warm night so Dexter put the top down on the Mercedes convertible. Birdie had brought a second car and had left to do some errands. So Dexter said, "Let's ride around."

By this time it was around 8:30 in the evening and the sun was setting in Charlotte. With a warm wind in our face we just drove for nearly hours. Dexter drove through one particular neighborhood and said, "This is where we had our first house. Our Glen Kirk house. This is where my kids really grew up in Charlotte."

He told me stories of what it was like to be in the Glen Kirk house. He pointed out how valuable the property was now. For nearly an hour we drove around that section of Charlotte and he showed me other properties.

He said, "You know I've been watching these properties. I've been driving around at night when no one is around. I love to operate late at night. I enjoy finding properties after dark."

He then said, "Let's look at some places on the lake."

It was 11:00 by the time we arrived at the lake. I know now what he was doing. He wanted to see what my "hot button" was. He wanted to see if I was interested in certain houses or investment properties or strip centers or lake front properties. He wanted to measure my reaction to these properties. He wanted to determine what I liked and what I did not like.

It was near mid-night and I was getting tired but I didn't want to miss anything that he said. We stopped and he reached under his seat and took out a long police style flashlight. It was a long, heavy gauge metal flashlight with a piercing beam of light. We got out of the car and he used the light to show me different details about particular properties.

And he said, "You know I love to do this at night because no one is around. I can take my time. Even though I'm not seeing it in the daylight this light is enough for me to see it. If I like it enough, then I'll come back during the day and see it from a different perspective. But I like exploring like this at night. I really enjoy this."

On this particular night I remember asking Dexter, "Well, how did this start for you? How did you begin staying up all night?"

"Well," he said, "I realize that people make a living from 9-5 and then after 5 they make a life."

I said, "What do you mean by that?"

He said, "What I mean is that so many people wait for the evening or weekend to do what they want to do. I decided to expand that into a lifestyle. I realized that at night the traffic is much less and there is so much more leisure time for me and the world is emptier. So I like to be with people and relax after their usual work schedules. People are much more relaxed after they've gotten off work."

He said, "I like that. But there is something more. Years ago, when I was first building my business and developing my dream with Birdie and my children, I would get in my car at night and drive around because I needed time with God. I needed to pray. With my relationship with Jesus Christ being the most real thing in my life I wanted to develop that. And so I found that these late night hours driving around were times of important spiritual development and times of great spiritual growth for me. These were times that I could drive around in the quiet of the night and hear God's still small voice speaking to my heart.

"I could also spend time thinking. There were so many levels of thoughts. I always understood that you cannot think something through with any depth, quickly. You need time to do this. You need time to develop your understanding. You need time to receive insight.

"So the late night hours when the traffic lessened and people went to bed I found that I fell in love with these nights. I fell in love with the quiet and the peace. I fell in love with the opportunity to unhurriedly seek God and think through my problems and challenges and situations and opportunities.

"Nights became later and later and I began to love it so much that I began to take the whole night, he said. "Now it is the life that I lead."

He looked at me with a twinkle in his eye and said, "Well, there is one more thing. Most of the meetings that I have done to build my multi-level business have also been at night. I sit with people at night and talk to them."

He called this his "night owl" sessions. I love that term because I am a night owl myself. As the evening goes on I rev up! I love the night. I'm not a natural morning person at all. So I related to what Dexter was describing.

He said, "We would have what I call 'night owl' sessions. I would sit up with people who were hungry for success. Hungry for knowledge. Hungry for business development. Hungry for income. Hungry for opportunity.

"Then after the business meeting would be over at 10:30 or 11:00 I would have these "night owl" sessions and they would go to 1 or 2 in the morning. Then I would drive to my next location and I would arrive there and sleep into the late afternoon. Then I would do another meeting in another city.

"So I developed a pattern of this. I began to realize that my desire for time alone with God and my desire for thought and calculation and examination merged logically with my business lifestyle and with my time with people after they would finish work."

He said, "You know, people are like onions. You just peel away layer after layer. I've found that the later it gets and the longer we spend, the more layers peel back and the more you arrive at the heart, soul and core of that person."

And he looked at me and smiled and said, "And you know, that's very special."

I didn't realize at the time that's what he was doing with me. But I could see him doing that with other people in these "night owl" sessions. He said in these "night owl" sessions was when the best questions would always arrive and the best insights would come. He said it was different than just being in a business meeting.

He also said, "I also found that those that would stay up with me at night usually were the ones who were the potential leaders. These were the men and women who had a greater desire for leadership. Even to the point where they would stay up late at night and persist into the early morning hours because they had such a desire for their life to be special.

He said, "You know Ron, I know God wants people to be loved and God loves them Himself. God wants them to know how really, truly special they are. So in these late nights I realized that I was picking jewels and gems out of the mix of dirt and rocks. The late nights were a way to sift through the dirt and the stones and the rocks to get to the diamonds and the pearls and the sapphires and the emeralds."

He said, "They didn't know they were jewels yet. They didn't know they were gems yet. But one of the indicators to me that they could be was their willingness to stay up with me after the business meeting at the "night owl" session and spend time expressing their hunger for something more. Something special. Something greater. I wanted to honor that."

So he smiled and said, "You see, there are many reasons why I stay up late at night."

I glanced at the clock in Dexter's car. We were still driving around and looking at properties as he talked to me. I noticed that it's 2:30 in the morning. I thought this is amazing! It's 2:30 in the morning. I thought surely he'll want to go to bed now. But he didn't. We went back to the lake house.

I remember for the next 4 or 5 hours sitting in his living room watching the sun slowly come up all over the water. I watched the geese skim the surface, the mist rising, the fish jumping. It was a magical moment. I suddenly realized I was having another dawn with Dexter. He was right. There was something intangible—something so unusual about that moment that I could sense it. I knew it. I knew that there was a quiet and a peace, not only with the time of night and the time of the day, but there was something about my relationship with him that had altered over the previous 2 hours.

When we had started around 2:00 the previous afternoon he had asked, "What are you doing? What are you dreaming? What are you reading? What do you want to talk about?" And I had eagerly given him lots of questions and answers. Now suddenly those questions and answers didn't seem that important to me. They didn't seem as valuable or meaningful to me.

I didn't realize it at the time, but a lot of my onion layers had been peeled off. Now I was sitting there watching the sun come up...a dawn with Dexter...and I realized I was ready to communicate with him on a level that surprised me. I was ready to listen to him on a level that equally surprised me.

So while the sun was coming up that morning...my second dawn with Dexter...I began to say, "You know Dexter, there are certain things that do concern me about my own life. There are people that I've had some challenges with. There are some situations that I don't understand. You know what you said about money last night and eating out? I eat out way too much."

He said, " Well Ron I figured you probably did because most people do."

I said, "Dexter the truth is I pick fancy restaurants because it's just entertaining to me. I pick expensive restaurants, not because I can afford them, I really can't. I pick them because it's recreational.

He said, "Are you sure that's all there is to it?"

I looked at him and I realized that the sun was coming up and another layer had just been peeled off. I said, "Well no Dexter. It's not just recreation. And it's not just entertainment. It's not just food. It's ego. I want to be validated by these restaurants. I want to have people look at me and see me in a restaurant like that. I want to be waited on in an expensive restaurant. I want to feel for a short hour or two that I'm somebody special."

He leaned forward and said, "Ron, you don't need that. You don't need the restaurant to prove that you're special. You don't need to be spending your money like that to reassure yourself of your own self esteem. I knew this would come up. It does with almost everybody. And I also knew that when it came up you would eventually see it for what it is. A self esteem problem. You've got a low self esteem problem. You don't think enough of yourself. So you want to have a restaurant prove to you that you're somebody."

He said, "Ron, you're somebody without those restaurants. You're somebody without that food. You're somebody without that expense and without that attention. You're somebody without any of that! You're somebody because God made you somebody. You're somebody because God has a purpose for your life. And we're going to find out more about that purpose. We're going to find out more about who you really are."

Then he said, "The first thing we're going to do before we go to bed..."

And at this point I'm thinking, "Go to bed! It's 7:00 in the morning." The dawn is fully up now and it's an absolutely spectacular morning. And Dex is talking about going to bed and getting some rest.

He looked at me and smiled and said, "The first thing that we need to do now that the sun is up is get you on the book again."

I said, "Well what is the book?"

He left the room and came back a few minutes later and said, "Here's my scheduling book. Let's book the next meeting together right now before I go to sleep and before you go to sleep. Let's book the next meeting right now."

So we looked at both of our calendars. We determined a time when I could go in and see him again and come back and spend another night and another dawn with Dexter. As I penciled in that date I felt a flush of excitement. I knew that I could hardly wait... wait for the next opportunity.

I went to one of the guest bedrooms about 20 minutes later and lay on the bed too excited to sleep. I remember looking up and saying a prayer, "Oh Lord, thank you for Dexter. Thank you for this time. Thank you for introducing me to a way of thinking and a way of living life that I never suspected was in existence. Thank you for giving me this friendship and I pray You will bless it and use it. Help me to have the wisdom to grow in this man's knowledge."

As I fell asleep that morning, the dawn was fully up, and I appreciated the fact that because of Dexter's lifestyle choices he had created bedrooms that were very dark with room darkening shades. As I drifted off to sleep I thought again what a privilege it was to be in this situation.

I woke up some hours later and the house was quiet. I realized that Dexter and Birdie were still asleep. I woke up around 12:30 in the afternoon and knew that I needed to drive back to Kentucky to Amy and to my family. I showered and slowly dressed and tip toed through the house. There on a table was a note from Birdie telling me where I could find something to eat. I opened the cupboard and gobbled down some high fiber cookies and some items that were on the shelf.

Then I saw another note from Dexter saying "Ron it was great! God bless you. Pull the door shut when you leave and it'll lock behind you. We'll see you next time."

I started to go and I thought, "Wait a minute. There is one more thing that I have to do."

So I walked back over to his study and I walked in and I just looked at the eagles one more time and prayed, "I want more of this. There's so much more that I need to know and need to learn. I want more of this."

I then left, already eager for my next dawn with Dexter.

CHAPTER 3

Know Your Players

The next meeting I enjoyed with Dexter was a month following the second visit. His schedule was full of appointments with people, so it was difficult for me to get back sooner. When I arrived in Charlotte I was eager to make up for the time I had missed.

I went to the lake house, as usual, and arrived there at the customary time of 2:00. I realized Dexter got to bed at dawn and he usually rose around 2 o'clock, so this would be a reasonable time for me to arrive. When I went in I was again met by Birdie, who asked me if I would like to sit for a few minutes because Dexter was on the phone.

I have since learned that Dexter, although he would block time for me, would frequently receive phone calls from individuals who wanted his attention, or needed his counsel, or sought his guidance on a particular matter.

I waited patiently. After about half an hour Dexter came in and was in his usual outfit of a t-shirt and gym shorts and old "run over" shoes. He looked as if he was bright and ready for the day.

I realized I was going to have another late night and another dawn with Dexter. I was prepared better this time having arranged my sleep schedule a few days prior to the visit so it would correspond better to his schedule.

I had my notebook and this time I had done something different. I had written down questions to ask Dexter. To my surprise I had ended up with 102 questions! I was nervous thinking Dexter would maybe not want to deal with that many questions in one visit.

I said, "Dexter I have a few questions."

Dexter said, "Well, how many? Can we deal with them in the next few minutes?"

I said, "Well, no. I have a lot of questions."

And he smiled and said, "How many?"

I said, "Dex, I have 102 different questions."

I was thinking that this would be too many. I figured Dexter would say, " Well Ron we could divide them up and maybe do a few this visit and then a few the next visit and a few more the next visit."

But to my surprise Dexter smiled an enormous smile. It was a mile wide grin and then he said, "Ron that's wonderful! I love that! It really speaks well of you that you thought of so many questions. Let's do your whole list...even if it takes us till," you guessed it, "till dawn."

I said, "Well Dex that's great."

Then he leaned forward and said, "Ron, you know, I've always operated on the foundation of knowing my players. Do you know what that means?"

I said, "Well I know what that means in sports. You understand the capacities and talents and temperaments of each player. You know who is more likely to respond to criticism or to praise. And who is more likely to get a hit or make a play."

Dexter smiled again and said, "Well you've got it. You have to know your players in business and in life as well. I make it my business to know the particular personality that I deal with. Really, my job for a number of years has been the management of egos.

"Now let me explain what I mean by that. I work with high powered, successful, driven, ambitious men. Men who are intelligent and dedicated and determined to make their mark in life. These are men who dream big and are always seeking higher goals.

"Because of that they sometimes have conflicting egos. I learned a principle years ago that I want to share with you today."

Now at this point I was still glancing at my list of 102 questions and was wondering if we really would get to them that day, or night. I looked up and Dexter was ready to continue, and so was I. So I listened.

Dexter said, "Ron, I always want you to remember this. There is a major difference between a big ego and a strong ego. A big ego is a problem. A big ego is a problem person who has to have his way and who is selfish and walks on people. A big ego is something I can not cure, because only God can. I cannot shrink that ego down to size. It is only for God to deal with that issue.

"But a strong ego is different. A strong ego is something everybody needs for success. A strong ego goes by other names. I know you recognize a few of them. One of them is self-confidence. Another is self-esteem. Another is self-belief.

"I want to point something out to you. You're from a church background. Is that right?"

I said, "Yes. That's right."

He said, "You've been a pastor and worked with one of my heroes Dr. Charles Stanley in Atlanta for a number of years.

I replied, "Yes that's right."

Dexter said, "Well, even a man like Dr. Stanley, or other great Christians leaders like Billy Graham, or Pat Robertson, or James Dobson...or Jerry Falwell," he concluded,—"All of them have strong egos. That doesn't mean they are bad men, or that they're out of the will of God. It means that they have strength of purpose and strength of commitment and strength of vision. They have such strength that they are not easily knocked off course when they face opposition and when they go through tough times and when they swim through seas of garbage. Their strong ego helps them because they believe in their calling and they believe in their mission and they believe in their determination."

He said, "You know I talked to a man recently who said, 'Some people think that when you give your life to Jesus Christ and you become a truly devout Christian that all your troubles are over and that it's smooth sailing from here on out. They believe they won't have another moment of anxiety and things are going to fall into place for you and things are going to be just great.'"

Dexter laughed a big laugh and he said, "Don't you believe it because that's when the devil kicks into gear. That's when the devil starts to throw everything at you. And that's why you need a strong ego. You need a belief that God has called you and a belief that God has positioned you and developed you and guided you and that your vision comes from God."

He said, "Look at my own life. When I started a multi-level Amway business, many years ago in Rome, New York, I lived in an alley. I had seven children and a wife to support. I had worked as a car salesman and I had worked in a store selling retail items. One day a man introduced me to the idea of Amway and do you think people patted me on the back and said 'Hey Dex go for it!'?

"No. People jumped on my case. They laughed at me. It was not easy, it was hard. I was a new and growing Christian and I was seeking God at the same time I was seeking how to succeed for my family. I was seeking how to succeed for future generations of Yagers who would come from Birdie and me. I knew I needed God's help, but I also knew that I needed a belief. A strong belief. A big belief. That's when I ended up having a strong ego."

He said, "It wasn't that I was egotistical, or self centered. At least I don't think I was. I tried not to be. I tried to have humility. But at the same time I knew that I could not let other people..."

(Here Dexter used a phrase that I since have learned is characteristic of Dexter. The phrase he used expresses a great deal of who Dexter really is.)

He said, " Ron I decided to not let anyone steal my dream. That's what I mean by strong ego. God could tell me to give up that dream and have a different dream. That would be different. But why should I let other people determine my future, or my income, or my success?

"So years ago I realized that I did not want a big ego. I didn't want to be somebody who had to be "molly-coddled" and someone people had to walk on pins and needles around me so they wouldn't offend me. I didn't want to be a tough guy like that who had to have my own way. But I knew I needed a strong ego. I needed the strength. I needed to have a commitment level that would not be thrown away or detoured by other people's negative opinions.

"So I came up with this idea. I decided I won't let anybody 'steal my dream.' Because that's what it is. It's theft. They're stealing something that God gave me. They're not going to pay my bills. They're not going to feed my family. So why should I make a decision based on a negative person's opinion of my business or my decisions. I'm not saying that I'm always right. I'm not saying I wasn't open to God leading me to something different. But, I did believe that God led me to the business and led me to the opportunity. When I prayed for God to help my small, growing family financially, He led me to a business! He led me to an opportunity. I knew that I needed a strong ego to be committed.

"So Ron that's what I mean when I say there is a difference between a big ego and a strong ego. You need a strong one, not a big one."

Now at this point the phone rang. I waited while Dexter excused himself and spent a few minutes talking to a man with intensity and concentration. Dex seemed to be very focused on the phone call.

After 20 or 30 minutes he hung up and looked at me and said, "I don't know if you knew who that was. That's a man who works with me sometimes. He's a very difficult person because he is very critical of a lot of things and a lot of people. He's having trouble with other members of his business organization so he called me to complain about someone."

He said, "Ron, I've already said that one of my key principles of life is to know my players. I know this man well enough to realize that his criticisms may not be sound. I know this man well enough to listen to him because he's very easily insulted. So I needed to listen with respect. I needed him to know that I was taking him seriously. But at the same time, when he criticized these other people in his group, I know this man well enough to realize that he may be over stating it because he does tend to be selfish. I listened to him, but if you paid attention to me on the phone you would notice that I did not commit myself to anything."

He said, "Let me tell you a story. I was having a meeting here once and two men came to see me. They stayed after the meeting and both of them asked me for financial counsel. I asked if both of them wanted to stay in the room together, or did they want counseling independently? Both of them said, 'No, it's fine. We don't mind the other being here.'

"So both men told me a story. Both men gave a description of a financial decision that each one wanted to make. Both men answered my questions and both men gave me the information I thought I needed to give them good counseling.

"Now in this case I did not know these men that well. They had been referred to me by what we call their upline, somebody above them in their multi-level business. I knew their upline well, but I did not know these men well. When I listened to them I took what they said at face value and gave them the counsel that each man required according to the information I had been given.

"Some weeks later, I found out that one of the two men, the second man, had done exactly as I told him to do. He'd been very successful. I'm not claiming credit for that, but God did allow me to give him good advice and he came out really good.

"But the first man, made a series of mistakes. Then he turned around and blamed me! Now he did follow my counsel. So when you look at it, it looks like it was my fault.

"But was it? I didn't know this player that well. I didn't realize that he'd lied to me when he told me his story. He lied about his financial situation and he lied about the circumstances related to this decision. I only gave him counsel based on what he told me. So based on the so called facts that he gave me, my counsel was right. It was not my counsel at fault, he was at fault. He lied to me and I gave him counsel based on those lies. The counsel didn't work and he blamed me.

"Now the truth is if he had told me the facts, and told me what was right, I would have given him different counsel. When I found out from his upline the true story, I realized that he had manipulated me.

"Now Ron, I will listen to a person so long. I will give them the benefit of every doubt. And I will try to trust them and believe them. But when I find out that they have lied to me, it's never the same. I could never totally trust them after that. They may come and apologize after that and make it right, but always in the back of my mind I will wonder 'Well are they telling me the truth this time?' In this case the problems that this man caused occurred, not because of bad counsel that I gave him, but because he lied to me in the first place. If I'd known my player better, that probably wouldn't have happened.

Then he leaned back and said, "Let me tell you what I do when I enter a room. When I go into a room, I size it up very carefully. If I'm speaking to a group that night, or just mingling among people to meet them, I will wait for a few minutes in a doorway trying not to be seen. I will watch everyone in the room for several minutes, carefully. I will try to determine who is more outgoing. Who is quiet? Who seems dependable? Who seems nervous? Who is hiding something? Who is open and expressive?

"I will look all over the room and I will say, 'I need to know my players. What are these people going to do? What are they like? How will they react to me?' I try to determine that before I ever enter a room."

He leaned forward and said, "Now again, that's what I mean by know your players. I'm getting to know you too. I know that you are nervous with me. I know that you are scared. I also know that you came from a church background. I don't want you to be offended by this, but there is a lot of socialistic thinking in churches."

When he saw that I looked surprised, he said, "You don't know what I mean by that, do you? Let me explain.

What I mean by socialistic thinking is there are a lot of people in the church who want something for nothing. They don't want to work for it. They don't want to earn it. They want to have people give them things that they don't deserve and they've not earned.

"You've come from that background. Preachers are notorious for wanting everyone to take them out to eat and pay the bill. I don't mind taking a pastor out and loving him, and rewarding him and paying his bill. But I don't think it ought to be expected. I don't think it ought to be demanded. I don't think the pastor should expect it every time just because he's a pastor. That's socialistic thinking.

"I think I know you and I know you are coming out of that. But I also know that you don't want to think like that. That you want to learn the principles of success."

He said, "I believe in America. I work all over the world. But I believe in what America stands for, free enterprise, an opportunity, hard work and reward for your labor. I believe in all that and I believe that you want to believe in all that. And that's one reason that I've decided to work with you. I believe that there's something in there and if we can get it out of you it can be something great and something special."

Now how do you think I felt at that point? I felt elevated. I felt inspired. I felt motivated. I felt on top of the world! This great man saw something in me and I was excited.

Then Dexter said, "Okay, what about the other stuff?"

I was confused and I thought, "What other stuff? What did I miss. What did I forget?"

I said, "Dex, I..."

He said, "No, no, no. What other stuff? Go ahead. I'm ready"

Finally I looked at him in panic and said, "I don't know. What other stuff?"

He said, "Your list. Your questions. How many you got? One hundred and two? Hey, let's go. Let's get them all in."

Some of my questions were quite simple and only needed a sentence or two to answer. Some were more lengthy. We were able to get through about 35 questions before it came time to eat.

Dexter said, "I'm hungry. Let's go get something to eat."

So around 5 o'clock we got into his Mercedes. It was the same one we had been in before. The top was down on a beautiful summer day. We drove with the wind whipping through our hair and his beard.

As we drove he said, "Now let's not waste any time. Let's do questions while we drive."

Here I am with the wind roaring in my ears and the scenery blasting past and trying to concentrate on my list as it flapped in the wind.

But Dexter said, "Come on. We gotta use our time. We gotta get these questions. You've got 102. We've only done about 30 or 40."

Actually we'd done 35, but at that point I was impressed that he realized approximately how many we had done. So I said, "Okay" and so I kept going through the questions. One after the other he would give me answers.

Dexter would give me something that helped me on every question. Even if he did not know the exact answer to the particular question asked, he would give me an insight into how to think about the question and how to approach the question.

I remember once that I asked him on that "wind whipped drive" about a man in his organization I had met. I said, "I don't understand this man. He smokes and he seems rough. Dexter you have a reputation for having a Christian based business and I'm not comfortable with this."

He laughed and said, "Well Ron, you've got to know your players. I know that man. I know he smokes. I know he's rough. But you don't know his background. You don't know how far he's come. You don't know what's happened to his life. He's asked Jesus in his heart. I know he has, I was there.

"Yeah, he's rough around the edges, but you can't just throw him out because he doesn't do everything right. He's smoked a long time. He's trying to quit. His wife wants him to quit. We're all praying for him. His health needs him to quit.

"I want you to know Ron that you don't take a guy like that and just throw him out because he doesn't fit everything you want him to fit. You just don't do that. You have to know your players.

"And I don't look at the smoking. I don't look at the surface. I look at where this man has come from, how far he's come, and I look at what he's doing in his life now. Now I'd like him to quit too, and I'm praying for him. But you don't know this man. You don't know how hard he's trying and I want to help him."

I began to realize that Dexter was very patient with people. He wasn't justifying smoking or bad habits, but he was recognizing that people started at particular places and needed to be developed from that point.

If fact, one of my later questions, around number 50, had to do with how you worked with people who bothered you and who you didn't like.

Dexter laughed and said, "Ron I work with a lot of people that I don't like. In fact, there are times when I think that all of the new people I work with are ones that I don't like. You know what? A lot of them don't like me! but if the dream is big enough, the facts don't count."

I said, "Dex, I've never heard that before. What does that mean?"

He laughed. By this time we were almost to the restaurant and we were pulling into the parking lot. We stopped and before we put the top up we sat there in the car with the motor idling for a moment.

He looked and said, "I'll tell ya, if the dream is big enough, the facts don't count. Here's what I mean. Let's say you got a big dream. You've got 4 men that can help you reach that dream, or 5 or 6. You need to work with those men and they need to work with you.

"Now let's say there are some places that rub you wrong and some things that you just don't like about each other. But you got a big dream. Your dream involves a lot of success and maybe a lot of money. Are you willing to temporarily forget those things that rub you wrong? Are you willing to just let it slide? Are you willing to forget it long enough to get your dream built? That's what I mean when I say if the dream is big enough, the facts don't count.

Because, you see, facts are what you make of them. I know there are two ways to look at facts. There are facts because they are just facts and they are true. But there is another way to look at it. Some people see facts and they are like real things. But they are made up in their own mind. These facts are things that get in their way. Maybe it's the fact of him smoking. Maybe it's the fact that he doesn't like you. Or the fact that you don't get along well together. Those seem like facts, but really you have made them up in your own mind. They're facts because they matter to you. Those are the facts I'm talking about.

"People think, 'I can't build a business.' 'I can't meet people.' 'I can't talk to people on the phone.' A lot of the people that come into our business are ordinary people. They're not people from big schools or big companies often. They're just ordinary, everyday people. To them the facts of their life are, 'This is as far as I can go.' 'This is all that I can accomplish.' 'I'll never do any more than this because this is as far as my dad went.' Or, 'This is as far as my education will allow me to go.'"

He said, "You see 'This is as far as you think you can go' are facts to you. But I'm telling you Ron, if the dream is big enough, those facts don't count. The fact that you don't like each other...those facts don't count. The fact that you only have so much education...that's a fact, but it doesn't count. The fact that you don't think you have a good enough personality to go out and meet people and build a business...that fact doesn't count. It doesn't count because your dream is bigger than that and you will change those facts. You will learn to work with those people that you don't like. You will learn to meet people when you're shy."

He said, "I was shy. I had trouble meeting people. This didn't come naturally to me. It was hard. It was harder than you know. But I just knew many, many, many years ago that if my dream was big enough, the facts didn't count. So that's what I'm saying to you. If you don't like these people and they don't like you, and your dream is big enough, the facts don't count."

Then he said, "I want to ask you a question. Have you ever been in a situation where you were doing something you didn't want to do, but the reward was worth it?"

I said, "Yeah, sure."

He said, "The reward was worth it, right?"

I said, "Right."

Then he said, "Then did the facts of how hard it was keep you from getting to your goal?"

I said, "No Dex they didn't because the reward was enough."

He said, "That's what I mean. The questions I always ask when I'm in a situation working with people is number one, 'Do I know my players?' and the other question I ask myself is, 'Is it worth it?'

"If I'm going to work with this guy, is it worth it? If I'm going to work with him and his wife, is it worth it? If I'm going to drive and see them, is it worth it? If I'm going to go and see this person and help them with their business, is it worth it? I want to tell you, if it's worth it, you keep doing it.

"And you know what I've found? Pretty much every time it's worth it. The few times it's not been worth it, I don't worry about that. Because the times it's not been worth it, when I've worked with somebody, I've sown seeds my own life and their life that will sprout in a way that God will surprise me with on down the road. I never worry about that."

"I'll tell you this," he said. "I never calculate what's in it for me."

I said, "What do you mean?"

He said, "Well, I don't go around saying, 'When I'm going to drive and see this man, I'm only going if he can guarantee that he's going to do this business with me.' That would be crazy. I'd be a fool. I don't know what he's going to do. I hope he's going to do something. I hope it's worth my time. But I don't focus on that. I don't concentrate on that. It would get me down if I did. I only think about the next person after him. And the next person after him. And the next person after him. And the next person after him.

"Yes, I want to know my players, but I need a lot of players. Because I realize that my business is a numbers game."

I said, " Well what do you mean by that?"

We're still sitting in the parking lot and the car engine is still idling. By this time I'm getting really hungry because it's 5:30 and

I'm wanting to eat. But I'm so focused on what he's saying that I don't want to miss a word of it.

He said, "Well, when you are in a position that your dreams can come true and you can know your players and you can work with people, there's so much more that you can do with your life. There's so much more that can happen for you. And what I was just talking about, let's pick that up later."

And he just dropped it right there. I found out sometimes Dex would decide that it was time to move on, and he would just move on.

So we got out of the car and went into a restaurant. Again it was not expensive, but he had researched and discovered it had really good food. So we went in and had just a great time eating and being with one another.

I went through more questions. I had already gone through 60, and this time I only had 42 to go. I was amazed at how he would be so focused on each question. I found out later that he told other people that Ron Ball had come in and brought a list of questions. 'Why doesn't everyone do that? I was touched by that and humbled and flattered and a little bit excited. I wanted him to think that I was making good use of his time, as well as my own.

After dinner he said, "Let's drive out again and look at some things."

We looked at cars and looked at different pieces of property. And just lots of things. The night became later and later. It's like peeling the onion. I began to realize more and more what he was trying to teach me and what he was trying to tell me about people. He had said earlier that it was a numbers business and that we'd pick it up later. Dexter I learned never forgets anything.

Around 10:00 that night Dexter leaned over and said, " Now, let me go ahead and explain to you a little more what I meant by this is a numbers business. I don't mean manipulation. I don't mean using people or trying to get numbers out of them. Or how many numbers of people you can get. That's not what I meant at all.

"What I meant is you need to work a business long enough till you find the leaders. Till you find the people with the magic and the magic touch. These are the people that you really, really want to work with. But you may have to go through 40 or 50 people to get to that one leader who is special."

He said, "I try to know my players well enough that when I get to that person I'll know who they are. I have friends in my business right now that it took me a long time to find them, but when I found them I knew I had something special. I knew that these people were worth mentoring and worth developing."

We were still driving around at 11:30 at night looking at property and he leaned over and said, "Let me ask you a question about Jesus. Didn't Jesus work with twelve men? Didn't he spend most of his time with those twelve men? Didn't he find twelve men who were worth his time and worth his investment?"

I said, "Well yes Dex He did."

He said, "What happened? He changed the world with those twelve men! I know that one of them was a loser and a failure. We won't worry about Judas, but look at what Jesus did through those other men.

"That's really all that I'm trying to do. I'm not comparing what I do to Jesus, but I'm sure trying to do what he does. I'm trying to find 10 men here and 5 men there and 6 men here and 2 men there who are special. I want to know my players. I want to find the men who can do what needs to be done. I want to find the men who will be worth my time and worth my investment.

"But I'm not going to be around that long. I'm going to die someday. Because of Jesus I'll go to Heaven. I want to leave something here that's real. I want to leave something that matters. That's why I've got you here tonight. I want to leave something in your life."

He said, "You've got a daughter named Allison."

I said, "Yes I do. You know about her?"

He said, "Yes. Because I know my players. Yeah I know about your daughter. I know you really love her. You've mentioned her when you speak publicly. So I know about Allison."

I have another child, named Jonathan, who was not born when I was first beginning to have my dawns with Dexter. But I did have Allison and she was a small child at that point.

Dexter went on to say, "Take Allison. If I can teach you something special; if I can imprint something into your life; if I can leave something spiritually successful in your life then you're going to pass it on to your daughter who will pass it on to how many generations of people? I don't know. There's no way to measure that."

I was just beginning to speak for Dexter at some of his functions and seminars and he said, "I also know that when you speak to people in church, or when you speak to people in my meetings, I want to transmit through you something to them that will change their lives. Something that will be permanent. Something that will change them forever.

"So here I am spending all night with you. Because I am doing this, I pray God will put something in you that you can use and can be used beyond you to many people you won't even meet."

So he said, "I want to know my players! I think you are a player worth investing in."

Once again my heart just jumped. My spirit soared. I thought, "He believes I'm worth that." I was humbled by that and I was hungry for more.

By this time it's after midnight. And Dex said, "Let's go back to the house and check on Birdie. He called her on his car phone and they chatted for a few moments. We drove into Dex's driveway and there was Birdie. She was getting a little tired. She goes to bed sometimes earlier than Dexter. So we visited with her for a few minutes.

The Dex said, "Let me show you something."

So we went into a room and there was a large screen television. It was hooked up to an early satellite system. This was back in the middle eighties when these systems were not that common. He had a huge, enormous dish that was big enough to take 20 people sliding down a hill if you wanted to snow slide with it. It was enormous.

We sat for almost two hours as he took a remote control and went from channel to channel from news programming to talk shows to sporting events. He would evaluate people on the screen. He went to Christian television. There were different TV evangelists and different ministers. He would evaluate them as well. Sometimes he would turn the sound off and say, "Just watch that guy. Just watch the body language. Watch his eyes. For two hours we would study people on different television programs. Then he would turn to me and say, "Now what did you learn? Who did you believe? Who seemed trustworthy? Did that guy on one of the religious shows come on too strong, or not? That sportscaster, did you trust him?"

It was fascinating to me how Dexter used something as simple as television watching to teach me how to know my players. How to understand people. How to discern their motivations and intentions. How to read their emotions and to understand the meaning of their body language.

By this time it's 2 0'clock in the morning and Dexter is going through detail after detail based on observation of these people. Then he surprised me and he got up and said, "Now you should have about 40 more questions to go. We gotta get those questions done. I'm hungry. Bring those questions and let's go get something to eat."

Actually I had 42 more questions and I remember driving in the car holding a flashlight trying to read questions. We got through 12 more on the way to an all night Denny's restaurant.

We went in to Denny's and everyone knew Dexter and everybody said hello to Dexter. He talked to the cooks in the back and he talked to the waitresses up front and he talked to the truckers sitting at the counter. After 15 minutes of talking to everybody we sat down and ordered breakfast.

By this time I had 30 questions to go. He said, "Alright, fire away!"

So I began to go through question, after question, after question, after question until finally I only had four questions left. By this time it is 4:30 in the morning and Denny's is buzzing around us and the early morning crowd is coming in.

So Dexter says, "Let's go back to the house and we'll do the rest of your questions."

So we arrived back at 5:00 in the morning. For the next couple hours we talked about four more questions because they were more detailed and more specific. Finally at 7:00 AM, on my third visit with Dexter, we finished my list of 102 questions!

I realized when I saw the sun rising over Lake Wylie that I was having another dawn with Dexter. I'd learned things that astounded me. I'd learned to know my players. I'd learned to observe people and pay careful attention to the way they acted and the way they responded and the way they projected themselves. Dexter had taught me so much again and had spent so much of his time with me.

Then I looked at the clock and it was 7:30. Dexter stood and stretched and said, "Well, I guess it's time to go to bed! What time do you need to leave?"

I said, "Well Dex it's fine. I'll leave later in the day and I'll get some sleep."

"Well your room's ready. The same room. I just need to talk to a couple people on the phone—unless you've got anymore questions?"

I said, "Oh Dex, 102, I've done 'em all."

He said "Okay. We're done with the questions."

He put his arm on my shoulder and said, "You know I like that. I think that's a good way to organize your time. That way we didn't waste any time at all, did we? Why don't you bring me some more questions next time. I like all those questions. Let's do it again."

Then Dex and I started to go when Dex said, "Wait. Wait a minute. I want to pray for you."

He put his arm around me and as well as I can remember he prayed this simple prayer for me.

"Dear Jesus, thank you for Ron. Thank you for Amy. Thank you for Allison. I pray that you will help the answers to these questions. Be what he needs. Give him a safe trip home tomorrow. Put your angels in charge over him. I plead the 91st Psalm over Ron. Don't let anything happen to him. I pray he will understand how big a dream you have for him. And as you've said in Your Word where two or more are gathered in Your name it shall be done. I claim that in Jesus name. Amen."

Then I prayed for him. I was so moved and touched. After a few minutes he said "good night" and left for another part of the house. Birdie was still asleep and he slipped into his bedroom.

I was so keyed up and the sun was sparkling on the water. It was almost 8:00 in the morning so I walked out on the deck. I just stood there. I stood on the deck and thought, "This is amazing! This is amazing that I have the privilege to learn these things from such a remarkable, influential and successful individual that also has a relationship with Jesus Christ. An individual that really wants to obey God. Who really wants to teach me! And I thought of Jesus and the twelve disciples. I felt a flood of humble gratitude sweep through me.

I looked up as the dawn was breaking everywhere and said, "Lord, I want to thank you for opening this door and allowing me this time. I don't know what will be the result of this for Amy, or Allison, or thousands of other people. I don't know what will come of this, but Lord I just want it to keep coming! I want it to keep happening."

I stood there looking at the water and watching the ducks and the geese. I assumed Dexter was already sound asleep in bed after making his phone calls. I just stood there soaking in the dawn and realizing all that I had learned and how remarkable it had been.

Finally I went to my bed. The room darkening shutters were already closed. I quickly undressed and lay there drifting off to sleep and thinking of the next dawn with Dexter. I couldn't wait.

When I got up later that day to leave there was the usual note: "Here's food. See you later."

I got into the car and I suddenly realized that I hadn't scheduled my next time. I panicked for a moment. I thought, "I can't wake Dexter up and I can't wait till he gets up because I had another commitment to go to. So what am I going to do?" I'd only slept 4 or 5 hours and I had to leave.

Then I remembered at midnight that night he'd be up somewhere. So I called till I found Dexter. I said, "I forgot...I need my next time scheduled."

Dexter said, " Ron I wasn't worried about it because I know my players. I knew you'd call. I was just waiting for you to bring it up. Uh, how about the thirteenth of next month? We'll do it again. Remember now, you bring all your questions and I'll be ready for you. Okay?"

I thanked him. I hung up and thought, "Wow! He knows his players. He knew I'd call and he was right."

And that was my third dawn with Dexter!

CHAPTER 4
The Secret of Humility

My next opportunity to be with Dexter Yager came almost two months after the visit just described. By this time I was beginning to know more of Dexter's patterns, and his procedures. When I arrived at the Lake Wylie home, I knew I needed to prepare a list of questions. Dexter seemed to like that. He recognized that that was an indication of the seriousness of our time together. He appreciated that I had spent the time to organize my thoughts in that manner.

So when I arrived I was proud of the notebook tucked into my briefcase. It was another spectacular day. I understood more and more why Dexter loved living on the water. There was a tranquility and a special dimension of life that was represented by the elements that God had created. The water was the wonderful expression of the positive healing atmosphere. I got to Dexter's house a bit early this time and just stood and looked at the water. I didn't want to go in for the first few minutes, because the scenery was so beautiful.

When I did go in Dexter had just gotten up. He was a little groggy and I discovered that he had been up even later than normal for him. He'd been up with a number of individuals the night before and had listened to their concerns and had offered them council. He had prayed for them until well past the dawn. So he was running even late for his schedule.

I had learned that often Dexter would have people night after night and day after day. There were some weeks that he would have no break at all. He would have men and women, husbands and wives, come in and spend time with him and Dexter would then council and pray for them. They would then depart and the next group would come in the next afternoon.

Well, I by myself was the next group that next day. This time I wanted to probe more deeply. I wanted to know what made Dexter tick. I knew that his focus was amazing, and I realized that his level of personal discipline was extraordinary. I wanted to understand what were his spiritual principles of life. As a committed Christian myself there was nothing more important to me than the discovery of God's effective life principles. I wanted wisdom. I hungered for wisdom. There's a verse in the Bible that speaks of hungering for God the way a deer hungers for water when it's heated in a chase. That's a good description of my perception at that point of my life.

There I sat with all of my questions. Dexter was taking a few moments to fully wake up. Birdie was walking around the kitchen organizing a light bite to eat. As I sat there I shot a fast prayer to God and said, "Lord, please make this the best time yet. Guide in detail what we do today, tonight, and in the morning.

After a few minutes Dexter smiled and said, "Well Ron, what do you have for me today?"

I began to go down my list of questions. I was already on question two when Dexter interrupted me and said, "Well how many do you have for me today? You didn't give me the count!"

I learned later that quantifying things was very important to Dexter. He liked to measure and monitor things. He liked to know "how much" and have an idea of what quantity was represented in any given situation. He liked to know how many people were at an event and how long did it last. How many points did this man have and how late did the meeting go? How long did it take to drive to the next meeting? He was always quantifying.

I learned later that was a way he organized his thinking. He liked to coordinate his thoughts in such a way that everything made sense to him. In that manner he could control, or organize, the flow of his activities. This was a way that he could always stay on top of his personal situations.

I said, "Dexter, this time I only have 98 questions."

Just as quickly Dexter said, "Well you had over a hundred last time!" and he proceeded to name the exact number.

I was impressed because I knew Dexter had already spent large amounts of time with numbers of people in the weeks since I had seen him. Yet he remembered that small detail. That's something else I learned about Dexter. The small details were very important to him. He believed that the right detail revealed the person and that if you were careful about the right details it was a good indication that you were alert to the situation that you were currently in.

Sometimes he tested me with that. He would say, "Well Ron how many questions last time? Do you remember what the 10th question was?"

He would always remember. I would sometimes have to scramble in my brain and think, "What was the 10th question last time?" I learned to take all my notes with me when I returned so that I would have something to refer to when he would ask me these questions "in fun."

I said, "Dexter I have 98 questions and we have just gotten through one and we're on number two."

Dexter replied, "That's great! We're going to have a fantastic day asking God to lead us."

Now when he said that I perked up. I thought, "WOW! He just said what I prayed. 'Lord guide our time together.'" I felt a sense of warmth and comfort with the realization that Dexter was focusing spiritually on the same thing I wanted. I felt a renewed excitement about the day together.

Birdie announced that she had prepared something light to eat. It was very simple. While we were in the kitchen the phone rang. Dexter leaned over and said, "Excuse me Ron," and answered the phone. After he had spoken for a few moments he put his hand over the receiver. Without any trace of ego, or pride, he calmly and in a matter-of-fact tone said, "Will you excuse me Ron. I know you have a lot of questions. This is Pat Boone on the phone and I just need to speak to him for a moment."

I said, "Well, yes! Of course. Please! Go ahead."

I left the room. I was excited that here was a man that would be receiving a call from a world renowned entertainer.

While I was there that same day, I noticed Dexter often received phone calls from remarkable individuals. In fact, that same day after the telephone conversation with Pat Boone, just as we were getting ready to go out in his Mercedes to go for a ride around the lake on this beautiful day, he received a call from the White House. The President of the United States had one of his assistants call Dexter to check on something. I was more amazed than ever. I thought, "I've been here for less than an hour and a half and Pat Boone has called; the White House has called; the President of the United States has contacted Dexter. What's left? What's next?"

During that particular day...the "phone call" day...Dexter received several other calls. I realized that there was probably a project that he was involved in that required contact with all these people. I was intrigued at the nature of the callers! These were remarkable and world-famous individuals. Each time a call came in Dexter would talk to the person very calmly, as if it was the most natural thing in the world.

Because of this, a small seed was planted in my mind. I knew that when the time was right, on this particular visit, I would need to ask Dexter probably the most important question I had yet asked him. But until that moment came and I knew that it was the right opportunity I shelved it in the back of my mind and waited.

We went to his car. We drove for 2 hours. Dexter loved to show me property. On this particular day he took the car down an old dirt road. We went as far as we could and then proceeded on foot to the edge of the lake.

Dexter said, "All this property is for sale. I also know the man who owns it. I am fairly sure you could get a good deal on this property. Are you interested?"

I said, "Well Dexter I don't know if I can afford it. It looks great. How much is it?"

He quickly said, "Well I happen to know that as well." He told me the price of the property and then he smiled and had almost a Santa Clause twinkle in his eye and said to me, "Remember, I know the owner!"

Then I realized that he was the owner. I said, "Dex, you own this right?"

He smiled and said, "Well yes I do. But I'd love for you to own it! Are you interested?"

I said, "Well, I'll talk to Amy and I'll go over the price and I'll see what we can do."

Now as it turned out, I did not buy that particular parcel of land but Dexter would usually on these visits show me properties that had great potential. In this case the property had the value of water front location. It was near another main road that would enhance the value of the poverty even more. In all the years that I have worked with Dexter and known him he has never shown me anything that would not benefit me in some way. There was always a plus for me. There was always an "up" side for me. To this day I appreciate how Dexter continually offered me opportunities that were good for me and would benefit me in some way. This particular day was no exception.

After we walked the property he showed me ways that the property could be developed. I was almost ready to leave, but I didn't want to say anything because I was his guest. Dexter continued to give me multiple ideas on how to develop the property. He was always brimming with practical suggestions. He would say "You could do this. You could move those trees. You could put this here. You could have a dock over there. This would create valve that would increase the poverty assessment. You would make more money if you did this."

He was always teaching me. Even while showing me lake front property he taught me and always encouraged me to think in practical terms that would create profit for me and my family.

After a certain amount of time, even Dexter got hungry and said, "Let's go eat."

Dexter had already communicated with me on other occasions his conviction that money should not be wasted on fancy restaurants and glamorous locations and expensive food. So, consistent with his principles, we again went to a country food cafeteria. It was clean; home cooked and lots of vegetables. It was great! Birdie drove up in her Mercedes and met us there. She was on the phone when she arrived and we waited a few moments in the parking lot until we all could go in. We sat down at a corner table after getting our food.

Dexter looked at me and said, "Ron why don't you pray for our food today." On previous occasions he had prayed.

I said, "I'll be happy too."

So I prayed. For some reason I sensed the need to pray for Birdie as well. So I prayed for her. I prayed for God to bless her and enrich her life as well. When I finished and the "Amen" was over, Dex and

Birdie looked at each other. Then both of them looked at me and said, "Do you know something?"

I said, "What do you mean?"

They said, "Birdie has been going through some challenges. There are some things that she has been concerned about. You just prayed for her in such a personal and sensitive manner that we thought, well, you must know something.

I said with some degree of embarrassment, "No. I just did what I felt in my heart was right to do."

They both smiled and I noticed they were holding hands underneath the table. These are individuals who have been married a lot of years with seven children and grandchildren. Here they are holding hands and Dexter was telling me, "Ron always pray for Birdie. Don't just pray for me. Always pray for Birdie. Always pray for her by name."

I could see how very much Dexter loved Birdie. I could see how he cared for her and protected her and cherished her. All that evening at dinner the conversation then flowed to a more spiritual focus and direction.

Dexter said, "Well here are more people you can pray for! You have your notebook. Right?"

I said, "Yes I do," and pulled it out of my small briefcase that I carried just in case we would cover the questions again.

Dexter named some other people to pray for. He had me write down sixteen names. Some I knew and some I'd heard of and some I didn't know at all. For each individual he gave me a specific statement. "Here's what he needs. Here's what she requires. Here's what would help her. Here's what would help him. Now you pray for them and we will together see what God does to intervene on their behalf."

I began to see again what a remarkable man I was dealing with. Here was Dexter Yager who had all these responsibilities. He was a man who traveled around the world and was incessantly busy. He was taking his personal time to give me individuals to pray for. He did it all from memory. He knew exactly what each individual needed.

In the previous chapter I mentioned his repetitive statement "Know your players." Here he was showing me again that he knew his players. I wrote down all the names and an excitement grew in me as I thought here was a man not only of great worldly wisdom and experience, but also a man of tremendous spiritual depth and insight as well. I wanted to know more.

Remember, there was a question that I had decided to ask him when the time was right. It was still walking around in the back of my mind. I had not forgotten it, but it just wasn't right yet. I knew I needed to wait a bit more.

We finished dinner and Dexter said, "Let's drive around some more. We got into the car and Dexter said, "What do you like to do? What do you like to see?"

I love bookstores. So that night for the first time he took me to some bookstores. It was great.

Then Dex said, "Ron I'm glad you enjoy this. Let me show you what I like to do."

He took me to a health food store. I had never been in a health food store before. I had seen them and heard of them. This was my first visit. Dexter went up and down the isles showing me different supplements and different items that would help me.

He said, "Ron, you're such-and-such an age and this will do this for you and this will help you with this. If you take this you will get this result."

He found about a dozen items that would help me.

He finally said, "Ron the biggest here is expensive, but I'm going to buy this for you. If you want the rest of them, you can get them."

I have learned in many years of working with Dexter that he never gives you everything. He may give you some things, but he wants you to create value for yourself. He wants you to personally invest in what you need. He won't do it all for you. No. He will give you a beginning, but if you want more you need to pay something. Dexter doesn't believe in Socialism. He doesn't believe in something for nothing. He believes in people paying their way and earning their own position. He doesn't believe in having "give aways" for things. It is his conviction that is an erosion of personal character. It is his belief that persons are diminished, devalued, and weakened when too much is done for them too freely and too quickly.

When Dexter offered to buy me this item that was priced for around $20 he also said if I wanted the other items it was up to me. I was already beginning to understand that this was his approach. If

71

this had enough value for me then I could get it for myself. Out of respect for him and also out of curiosity as to the promised benefits of some of these items, I bought several more myself. We put them altogether and placed them in the trunk of his car and then we went driving to some other places he wanted to show me.

He wanted to show me boats. We went to one place just as the sun was setting. The evening was arriving and the sunlight had been clear and refreshing all day. Now the sun was setting in spectacular shades of reds and pinks and purples. We arrived at the boat dealership. It was a dealership for houseboats. These were large boats that some-one could easily live on indefinitely. They had kitchens and bath-rooms and some of them with fireplaces and Jacuzzis! They were impressive.

Dexter said, "Let's look at some of these houseboats."

We climbed on board several of them and just as we were going up one of the boat's ladders, a man appeared and said, "Dexter! You're back!"

Dexter daid, " Well, hello. Yes and I brought my friend. This is my friend Ron. He's a minister. He's going to look with me at some of the boats."

The man smiled and said, "Well Dexter we are getting ready to close, but that doesn't count for you! You stay as long as you want. There's a security gate you can go out. You can't go in...but you can go out. You stay for as long as you want and if you want any of the boats opened I'll open them for you. You just tell me whatever you want to do, and I'll do it."

I've since discovered that responses like that to Dexter were com-mon. People trusted him entirely and totally. Not only did they trust him, they liked him. They would allow him to do things that they would not allow anyone else to do.

That night after the staff left the houseboat dealership we contin-ued for another hour and a half. We looked at many boats and we opened up chambers and different rooms on the various boats. I noticed that Dexter did not just show me boats, or try to impress me with these things. No. He taught me again. He would teach me things about the boats.

He would say, "Ron you want this in a boat, but you don't want that." "Ron, do you see how in this particular boat how glamorous this looks? But you don't need these because they are money for nothing. You will never get the money back. You will never get a return on your money if you buy a boat with these things in it because they are wasted and just glamour. You can put them in more cheaply later if you really want them, but don't buy them with the boat."

He took me to another boat and said what I really needed in a boat were different types of equipment. He said, "You need two of these and then this will be a much better investment for you."

These boats were more than my house. I was not even thinking in terms of investing in one of these boats, but I was interested that Dexter was still teaching me. He was teaching me what boats were good and what boats were not; why to buy this one and why not to buy that one; explaining why this one would be of more benefit than that one.

One thing that Dexter kept emphasizing was how to get more for your money. He would continually stress this one fact. If you'll do something right you'll get more financial benefit out of it. He said if you're not impulsive and you don't buy out of emotion, you will benefit even more.

He said something to me that evening that I've never forgotten. He said, "You make money not when you sell something, but when you buy it."

At first I was puzzled. I asked, "What do you mean Dexter?"

He said it again. "You make money not when you sell something, but when you buy it. What I mean by that is that if you want to put yourself in a position to make a reasonable, honest profit on something you need to first buy it right.

To buy it right? I thought, "Now what does that mean?"

He could see the look on my face and he said, "What I mean is you need to negotiate the lowest price. You need to get the best value for your money. You want to buy features on the boat, or whatever item it is, that other people will want. You don't want to buy something that is so high end in glamour that most people cannot afford it. You want to think all this through. The most important thing to remember is don't ever, ever go to look at something and go with the emotion that you have to have it."

He went on to explain, "You are in the grip of the salesman. He will control you if he senses that you have to have it. He will know that you won't be very negotiable because you've already made a mental choice. You've already made a decision. You've already decided that you want that item. Because you've already decided that you want that item you are vulnerable. You are weakened in your position. Because you want it so much, the salesman will know that all he has to do is nudge you in a certain direction and you will probably take the plunge. The best thing to be able to do if you want to buy something and buy it right and the cheapest way possible is to go in and not have to have it at all. The most important thing you can do is to decide before you go that you can walk away from it without any problem at all. If you don't have to have it and you can walk away from it, the power moves to you. The power is no longer in the hands of the person selling it. The power now belongs to you because you're the buyer and you can now leave when you want. If you leave saying, 'I don't need this,' the deal will get better and better."

Dexter went on to explain, "You may be wondering what if the deal doesn't happen? You may walk away and the salesman does not come back to you or offer you a better price or a better term. You're thinking that aren't you Ron?"

I said, "Dexter as a matter-of-fact I am. What if it doesn't work?"

He smiled the biggest smile and said, "If it doesn't work...who cares? Big deal! Here's the other thing to remember about buying something, Ron. There is always another deal. There's always something as good, or better. Always. Not some of the time. Not most of the time. All the time. There is always something as good, or better somewhere. You're never obligated. You're never locked in. You're never in a position where you are trapped into buying that particular item.

This had been a remarkable education for me. I had been one of these guys who would walk into a car lot and drool over the car and have to have it. I had to have everything on it and had to have every bell and whistle available. I'd have to have the hottest color they had. I would want that car so badly that I was an easy mark for most salesman. I would go into a store and have to have a particular type of clothing. Or I would want a certain something and I would have to have it and I would imagine owning it, That would make the value grow in my thinking. My emotions would already be bonded to that item before I even got there. I was a sap many times. I bought things that I could not afford and created debt that was stupid and foolish for me.

Dexter was training me. He was disciplining me. He was teaching me. All we were doing on the surface was looking at houseboats at a dealership where the staff had gone home. We were just walking through boats casually as Dexter made comments and pointed out particular features. But Dexter was continually teaching me important financial lessons.

I will never forget what he taught me. Dexter was always doing this. He still does this. He teaches at every available opportunity. He is always looking for the heart and core and essences of something. He's always thinking in practical terms. How do you get this out of this. How do you benefit here. He is so down to earth practical I can't think of anyone I've ever met that is like him.

That evening after we left the houseboat dealership, we drove around the lake and looked at more properties. I have since learned that there are always more properties to see. We never ran out. We never lost opportunities for more visits to more properties. That night was no exception.

We drove well past midnight until Dexter finally said, "You know I'm hungry."

We went back to the all-night Denny's that we had been to before. Again, everyone knew Dexter and for 15 full minutes, Dexter would greet people and go in the back and talk to cooks and those who were flipping burgers on the grill. He also walked down and talked to the manager for a few minutes. After that 15 minutes he'd conversed with almost everyone in Denny's!

By this time it was 1 o'clock in the morning and Dexter said, "Well how about an early breakfast?"

We ordered eggs and pancakes. At this point in Dexter's life he ate in a way that he doesn't eat now. He would order pancakes and different kinds of high calorie food. He doesn't do that anymore. Dexter had a remarkable physical transformation in the last few years. H now eats in a very balanced and smart way. He's in tremendous physical condition and he works out at a gym regularly. He has transformed himself physically.

But back then we both ate late at night and this night was no exception. So at 1 o'clock in the morning I was ordering pancakes with Dexter, with extra syrup. They had cheese eggs. I said to Dexter, "I love cheese eggs. Why don't you get some too?"

Dexter said, "Nope. I'm allergic to cheese. I can't eat cheese at all. No cheese."

I said, "That's great." I made a metal note that Dexter was allergic to cheese and to stay away from cheese for Dexter.

We ate for about an hour and talked. By this time it was 2:30 in the morning and Dexter and I made our way back to the lake house.

At several points in the evening Dex had called Birdie, or Birdie had called him. They had coordinated where they were and what they were doing. Birdie was at the house having a late-night massage. A wonderful lady had come to their home and was giving her the massage before she went to bed. Birdie had called just minutes before we reached the lake house and told Dexter the massage was due to begin and she would see him later that morning when they both got up.

So Dex, having checked on Birdie assured himself that everything was in order, drove for a few more miles and looked at a handful of properties and then we arrived back at his lake house. We came in the side door and were careful not to disturb Birdie in the bedroom with her massage therapist. We slipped into Dexter's study and Dexter said, "Ron I'm going to take a couple minutes and check some messages. Is that okay?"

I said, "Fine."

During the last few hours I had been going through the list of 98 questions with Dexter. I had asked him questions on financial matters and personal situations. I had also asked him his opinion of world events and political leaders. I asked him about everything I could think of. Every question that I could think of in the previous two weeks was on that list. By this time, out of 98 questions, I was already at 78. I had 20 questions to go and it was already 3:00 in the morning. As Dexter checked his messages, I decided to sit with my list.

Now I wasn't entirely accustomed to Dexter's schedule. I began to become drowsy while I waited for Dexter to finish checking his voice mail. At about 20 minutes into his messages I suddenly woke up. I had dosed off and I was embarrassed. Dexter paused for a moment while he checked the messages and looked over at me and said, "Hey Ron! Go to sleep if you want. I'll wake you up when I'm done."

Dexter was always flexible and was never judgmental. I thought, "Why not." I leaned back and drifted off again until suddenly I realized that it was raining. I couldn't understand why it was raining. I gradually came awake and realized that it was not raining, but someone was dripping water on my face! There was Dexter, full beard and all, like a kid in school with the biggest grin dripping water on my face and laughing all the time.

He said, "Hey! We got 20 questions to go. Come on let's go!"

By this time it was about a quarter to four in the morning. My questions were very simple at this point. I'd arranged the easy ones toward the end and so I was able to go through about 10 questions in 20 minutes. Just a little after 4 o'clock in the morning and I had 10 questions yet to go. But I knew this was an unusual opportunity for me and I had decided to add a particular question to my list some hours before.

I said, "Dexter, I have another question to ask you. I have something that is more important than my 10 remaining questions. I want to ask you very, very honestly to give me an answer on something of great importance."

Dexter said, "Sure." He leaned back and put his feet up and said, "Fire away."

I said, "Dexter, when I arrived earlier you received a series of remarkable phone calls. Pat Boone. The Whitehouse. The President of the United States. Calls from a number of leaders who are well known throughout the country. I know that you make a lot of money. I know that people on that level call you personally. I know that you have great world influence because I have been able to see it myself. Having been here today I have witnessed even more the connection you have of great people. So I want to ask you a question. How do you stay on track?"

Dexter said, "What do you mean by that?

I said, "I mean how do you stay on track spiritually? I mean, how do you stay humble before God? I mean most people have egos out of control. They are sometimes dominating and arrogant. Yet spiritually you treat people so wonderfully. I've watched you in the Denny's talking to the cook in the back and the waitress up front. I watched you at the dealership that sold houseboats how thoughtful you were to the night watchman before he closed up. Dexter, you treated him with respect and were never uppity. You were never difficult. Yet you have phone calls from entertainers and the White House. You have all this money and influence. How do you do it? How do you stay on track? How do you keep a humble attitude before God?"

Dexter took his feet down and leaned forward and said, "Now that is a question that deserves a real answer. How do I do it?"

Dex had to think for a minute. I realized that Dexter wanted to give me an answer that really meant something. He didn't want to give me a throw away comment off the top of his head. He wanted to give me something that mattered. I wanted it. I wanted to know how do you stay humble in a situation like this?

"Ron," he said, "I'll tell you what I do. I do certain things everyday. I never miss them. I think this may be the answer to your question. Here's what I do.

"Every morning when I wake up I remind myself that God doesn't really need me. That God is so big that He can do anything He wants without me. In fact, the way I do it is like this. I always try to see myself from God's point of view. I always try to see myself the way God sees me. If I look at myself through God's eyes, I shrink down to a very small size. I'm not that big. I'm not that important. I'm not that unusual. I'm just little me. When I look at myself through God's perspective it shrinks me down to my right size. God doesn't need me. If He uses me I'm happy. If He speaks through me I'm glad. But I know He doesn't have to have me. I always remind myself of that.

"But I do something else also." He said, "I always remind myself when I get up in the morning that people are depending on me to be the 'real deal.' People count on me to be genuine. People depend on me to be trustworthy. They depend on me to be Christian and honest. They depend on me to be who I claim to be. Because they need me to be that, I don't ever want to fail them. I don't ever want to let them down. I don't want to disappoint them."

He looked at me intensely and continued. "So everyday when I wake up I ask God for the same thing. 'Lord, don't let me disappoint anyone. Don't let me let anyone down. Don't let me do something that would make people not believe in You. Don't allow me to do anything that would hurt anyone else.'"

By this time he had leaned back with his arms behind his head. He said, "I guess that's about it. I try to see myself from God's point of view and I also try to remind myself that people need me to be the real thing spiritually. I ask God to help me do it. I guess that's it."

I said, "Dexter, what about other people? You work with diamonds. You work with other leaders in your multi-level business. They are just amazing individuals. I had met a number of them and had been deeply impressed with their professionalism and their commitments and their discipline and their hard work. How do they stay humble? What do they do?"

Dexter unlocked his hands and leaned forward toward me. "Ron," he said, "I've only seen diamonds and leaders fail for two reasons."

By diamond he meant the high levels in his business. Those are the people making the significant income. Those people have large numbers of people under them. They have leadership positions in the multi-level organization that Dexter was affiliated with.

He continued. "After all their successes, I've only seen them fail for two reasons. For two reasons I've seen them mess up and lose what they have. Now those two are pretty serious. They're big ones."

I said, "Dexter please. What are they?"

He said, "Yes. There are only two reasons I've seen people fail after they succeeded; after they have made commitments to Christ; after they have built a good people business. By the way, do you know what I mean when I say a good people business?"

I said, "I think so."

"Just to be sure," he said, "this is what I mean. I mean a business that loves people. A business that puts people first. I can't do anything for anyone if I don't love them. I can't help anybody if I don't care about them. People have to come first. Their needs have to come first. So if one of my guys puts together a business and succeeds with it by caring about people and loving people and putting people first, and then starts to lose it and fail and starts to lose God's blessing...well, in my experience there are only two reasons that happens."

By this time it is nearing 5 o'clock in the morning and it is deathly quiet on the lake. I am utterly focused on every word Dexter is saying. I wanted to know what he's about to say.

He looked at me with intensity and he explained, "Ron the only two reasons I've seen people succeed and then fail are cockiness and greed. Think about it. Cockiness. That's when you believe your own publicity. That's when you get full of yourself. That's when you're a hotshot. you're a big shot. you have to be taken care of. You are on some kind of false and phony pedestal. You're the center of attention; at least in your own mind. Here you are, cocky, arrogant, easily insulted, overly sensitive and wanting people to take care of you."

He said, "What's greed? Greed is just selfishness in another form. Greed is wanting something that you haven't earned. It's wanting what other people have when you don't deserve it. Both reasons go together to ruin a man or woman's life. Think about it. Cockiness and greed."

I had been working on a special project that Dexter knew nothing about. It had to do with an understanding of today's celebrity culture. People are obsessed with celebrity lifestyle; with celebrity hair style; with celebrity marriages and divorces. It's as if the celebrity has a life in Technicolor while the rest of us somehow struggle along in black and white. But listening to Dexter I realized something that morning. I realized that there is a gigantic difference between a celebrity and a hero.

A celebrity may be famous and may receive a great amount of attention. He may be surrounded by hoards of people. A celebrity may be toasted and placed on a pedestal as Dexter described. But that does not mean that the celebrity is a hero. It does not mean the celebrity is a good man or a good woman. It does not mean the celebrity has Godly, positive, helpful influence on other people. Dexter was saying that sometimes a leader, even in his own business, could become a celebrity figure. He could become full of himself. Through cockiness and greed, he can begin to ruin not only his own life, but the lives of the people around him, and especially his own family.

As Dexter was talking, I remembered that research. I knew that here was a man that was well known, influential, respected, highly thought of, but he was not just a celebrity figure. he was more than that. He was a hero. He was a man who sacrificed himself for every-day people. He was a man who never forgot that he came from an alley in Rome, New York. I realized that here was a living, breathing example of what I was talking about. Dexter was an example of what

I was researching. He was a living, breathing example of a hero, not a celebrity.

As Dexter finished, I snapped back into focus and looked at him and said, "Dex, this may have been one of the most important things you've ever told me. To put people first. To not be a full-of-himself celebrity. To be someone who really loves people and loves God and gives his life to help."

Dexter said, "Isn't there a verse in the Bible Ron that says something about losing your life?" He smiled.

I knew that he wanted me to come up with it. He was always stretching me and testing me. After a moments thought I had it.

"Yes Dexter," I said. "Jesus said that if you lose your life you find it. It's like a seed that falls into the ground. The seed dies but then the seed through death produces an awesome harvest."

Dexter said, "That's it! I want to be one of those men whom God uses to produce an awesome harvest."

By this time it was 5:30 in the morning and the sun was just beginning to peak over the edge of the water. I had 10 questions yet to go and I hurriedly went through them because I knew Dexter wouldn't quit or stop or sleep until those questions were dealt with. Until 6:30 in the morning I went through the other 10 questions.

However, I kept thinking what he had said about cockiness and greed. I thought of myself and prayed, "Lord I don't know what You'll ever do with me, or what You'll ever want to do with me, but I pray that You will protect me from what Dexter just described. Please protect me from cockiness and greed and that I'll never be selfish or self centered. I want to be a giver. Lord thank you for bringing Dexter Yager into my life. I need to know what he knows." I remember praying that prayer in Jesus' name as we were finishing up my questions.

Then it was 7:00 and all too quickly 7:15. Dexter said, "Well...it's about time to get some sleep and you have to drive home in a few hours. Right?"

I said, "Yes Dex."

Then I looked out and saw the full, spectacular dawn over the lake and I thought, "WOW! Another dawn with Dexter. This is more than I ever expected and more than I ever dreamed of. I could not wait for the next time.

I said, "Dexter, where's your schedule book?"

I'd learned my lesson from the earlier visit not to leave without the next date.

I said, "I want to get on your schedule now."

Dex grinned his big grin and said, "I knew you were learning!"

He got his schedule book and we picked a date. I knew that I could hardly wait for my next dawn with Dexter.

CHAPTER 5

Keep Growing!

I was already looking forward to my next dawn with Dexter. I was astounded at the changes that had occurred in me whenever I would be with Dexter. I would arrive home and Amy, my wife, would be impressed with what I had learned and would frequently comment on the new attitude I had towards success and the new hunger for God that I enjoyed. She said these times with Dexter were well worth the investment; well worth the opportunity; well worth the time. She always encouraged me to make sure that I spent time with Dexter at every available opportunity.

Once when I had arrived home from Dexter's, I'd had something of an argument before I'd left. When I got back I immediately went to Amy and said, "Amy I want to apologize. I'm so sorry for what I said before I left."

Amy said, "Well why are you apologizing now?"

I was very honest. I told her, "Because I saw the commitment that Dexter had to Birdie and I want that kind of commitment to you. I also always want to show you that level of consideration."

Amy was enthusiastic in her support of my dawns with Dexter.

When the next time arrived on the schedule for me to make a visit, Amy and I took a few moments to pray together for God to give unusual direction and blessing to this visit. When I arrived it was in the fall and the weather was not as nice. It was windy and cool, but still beautiful on the water. I realized every time I came that Dexter was right about the atmosphere that water created. There was something creative and special about being in such a location.

I arrived and everything was as usual. I was beginning to recognize the patterns that Dexter and Birdie followed. When I arrived I was not surprised that Dexter was still asleep. I was there a few minutes before 2 o'clock and I wasn't surprised either that Birdie was in the kitchen and was just beginning to put some food items out for a snack.

Don't misunderstand me. Birdie did not cook for me. I never saw her make a meal during the time I was there, but she always had something available in one of the cabinets that would be a good snack until we could go somewhere to eat outside their home.

On this particular occasion Birdie was getting some snacks ready and Dexter was a bit late coming downstairs. I just waited. I remember going back to his office. This was the one with all the eagles everywhere. I sat looking at the water and looking at the eagles thinking, "What an amazing way to live!"

I noticed that since my last visit, Dexter had added a guest book.

Birdie had asked me to sign it when I came in, so I did. While I was waiting I began to flip through the pages of the book from the previous few weeks since I had been with Dexter. Every page was filled with someone. There were people from all over the world. I realized that Dexter had not had one day off or one break sine I'd last seen him. He was mentoring people from different locations and different backgrounds. He was doing this everyday. I felt even more honored that I had the opportunity to be with him and be mentored as well.

After a few minutes of waiting and anticipating, Dexter arrived in the study. As usual he was in a t-shirt and shorts and an old pair of shoes. I could tell that he'd had a particularly late night, or should I say early morning. I found out that he'd had a group stay over a bit longer than planned. It was now around 3 o'clock and Dexter was just arousing himself to get going for the day.

Dexter sat in a chair across from me in the study and said, "Well how about it Ron? Do you have any questions for me this time?"

Of course I did have questions and I said, " Well Dex I don't have nearly as many questions as last time. I only have 67 questions this time.

He said, "Oh! You're dropping down. You had much more the last time. Nearly one hundred and you had over a hundred the first time.

Are we answering all the questions or are you not thinking of as many things to ask me?

I smiled and said, "Well Dexter maybe it's a little bit of both. But I do have 67. We can go through them one by one.

Then Dexter said that one reason that he was so excited about me bringing questions was because he was committed to growth. I was intrigued by this so I asked him to say more about it.

He said, "Well it's very simple. If you stop growing you start dying. If you stop developing you begin to go backwards. It's like a car. If you put a car in gear and start going up a hill and you suddenly take your foot off the gas and just sit there, the car is going to start going backwards. I always keep my foot on the gas of my life. I'm always putting more fuel in so that I can accelerate more. Let me tell you how that fits goal setting for a moment."

I realized that we were about to enter into another series of comments about things that I needed to learn. I put my list of questions aside and sat and waited and listened as Dexter explained how goal setting and fuel and growth were all intimately related.

He said, "For example, I always have goals ten years ahead. I have five different categories or areas. I have goals in each of those areas going ten years into the future. If I don't keep growing in all five of those areas I know immediately that something is wrong. I use those goals to keep me motivated. I have financial goals and personal goals and spiritual goals. I have 5 very specific areas. Each of those goals involves my growth.

"Let me give you another example. I'm very thankful to God for this, that I'm at a point in my life that if I want to go out and buy a new car or boat it's not a big deal. It's not a hard decision. I can go out and buy the boat or car without any debate or consideration because I have the money to do it. But I don't let myself do that. I know that it would "de-motivate" me.

"Here's what I mean. If I go out and buy what I want and when I want, it will soften me. I will not be as sharp or aggressive. I also won't be as committed to growing or helping other people grow because I will get what I want too easily and quickly. What I do is very simple. I will know that here is a car that I want. I will not allow myself to have that car until I grow my goals in one particular area. Once I grow my goals in a big way I'm not going to fool myself, or trick myself, or lie to myself, or take advantage of myself. I want to tell me the truth more than anybody else. So when I tell myself the truth and say, "Dexter, here is a goal that you will have to stretch and grow to get there. Then I will say 'There's my goal for my car!' I will use the car which I could have bought anyway at any time as a reward for me achieving that goal in that area or that category."

He said, "That's why growth and rewards and goals are all connected and related. That keeps me motivated. That keeps me fired up!"

When he said those words I looked up. I had heard a lot of people around Dexter use the phrase "fired up!" Dexter himself had used it on several occasions. I realized that this phrase summed up his attitude. He wanted to stay "fired up" about life. He wanted to stay "fired up" about commitments and about goals.

He then said, "You know Ron, people talk about retirement. I don't ever plan to retire because I love what I do. My whole purpose in life is not to make money, but it's to help people. If I can mentor people and help people grow and help them learn from my mistakes and help them learn from what I've gone through—then that's God's purpose for me. That's a joy for me. That's a fulfillment; a satisfaction; a happiness for me.

"It's very simple. If I want to help other people grow I need to keep growing myself. I need to keep moving forward and I need to keep advancing. If I don't do it, how can I expect other people to do it? So I always want to stay "fired up!" I always want to stay motivated.

"Look at the retirement question again. People say 'When I retire I'll do something with my life.' I want to do something with my life right now. I don't want to wait for some unknown retirement that I may not even live to see. I want to work hard now so that I can fulfill my dreams now."

He went on to say, "My dad, who was a plumber in New York state, always told me that Yagers don't work for other people. Now what did he mean by that?

"He didn't mean that Yagers wouldn't help someone else or do a job with someone else. He meant that they lived their life in such a way that they were their own boss. They owned their own business. He was plumber and had his own plumbing business. Early on my dad poured into me this idea that you need to own your own business. I realized early with my Amway opportunity that this was the chance to do the dream that my dad had built into me. If I did that and kept growing, then the rewards would come. The goals would be achieved. I then wouldn't have to worry about some retirement down the road, I would be living the life of my dreams throughout my life."

At this point I had started taking notes because I realized that Dexter was on a roll. He was going to give me information that was going to be beyond what I had gotten in the past. I wanted every word and every syllable of what he had to say. So I just sat there and took notes as he continued.

He said, "Look at the whole idea of a mid-life crisis. Men are saying that at times they struggle. They think they have missed out in life. They are in their forties and they want a hot, red sports car. They want to leave their wife, children, family to find themselves. I've thankfully never had that problem because I live the life of my dreams and I don't have any regrets. I've gone for everything that I've wanted. Everything that I've ever wanted I've gone for. I've reached for it. I've tried for it. Sometimes I've failed. I've missed my goal. But I've always tried for it so I've never had regrets. I believe because I've never had regrets, is why I've never had a mid-life crisis."

Then he laughed an infectious laugh and said, "You know, I really wouldn't have time for a mid-life crisis, would I? I have too much to do. Too many people to help."

He laughed again the heartiest, most healthy laugh and smiled again and said, "Hey, let's go get something to eat and we'll talk about this some more. But I'll tell you, no mid-life crisis for me. I just ain't got time."

We went to the other room and Birdie was ready. We got into two cars again so that Birdie and Dex would have the freedom to go where they needed to go after they ate. They would then not be obligated to each other's schedule and they could have flexibility. We went to the cafeteria where we had eaten last time. We piled our plates with vegetables and had a wonderful time talking and laughing.

By this time I realized that there had been a change at the cafeteria. The change was not in the cafeteria, but the change was in the reaction of the people in the cafeteria to Dexter and Birdie. Everybody who worked in the cafeteria, and many of the patrons who ate there, all seemed to know Dexter.

That had not been true on the two previous visits. But apparently something had happened since our last visit and Dexter and Birdie were welcome like old friends and family to this public cafeteria. People would greet Dexter and Birdie and give them a hug and say "How you doin'?"

I realized that Dexter had created this situation. He and Birdie had shown such friendliness and openness to these people. They had taken time to meet the managers and owners. They apparently had brought other guests in as they had brought me. So everyone was happy to see them. Dexter was adding to the bottom line but he also was so much fun to be with that everybody responded to him in a positive and welcoming manner.

While we were eating people would come over to Dex and Birdie and speak to them by name. These were men and women who had been total strangers to them just weeks before and now seemed to know them well. The secret I knew was in Dexter and Birdie. They were the ones who had opened their hearts and minds and had pursued relationships with these total strangers.

I could see that Dexter was making a difference wherever he went. That's what he'd told me on more than one occasion. He'd said, "Ron, I want to make a difference for God in the lives of other people before I die. I want to make a difference so they will be better because Birdie and I came through their life. People suffer from low self-esteem. Because of their low self-esteem they are afraid to talk to other people. They are reluctant to contact strangers and they want to wall themselves up and keep themselves separated from other people whom they do not know. My purpose is to break through that wall and break through that barrier. I need to make a connection with these people and love them and show them God's love."

Here is this multi-millionaire. Here is this man who has great wealth, power, influence who is excited and motivated because he is in a position to influence the lives of people he's never even met before.

Dex continued saying, "Ron I believe everybody has a dream

buried within them. That dream will transform their life if it can just get out! I just want to be the helper to get the dream out. I just want to help get it to the point where it can start changing them. I want them to see who they are and that God made them and that God didn't make a mistake and that God wants to use them. That just motivates me more than anything in the whole wide world."

The cafeteria experience was also a teaching opportunity. I was beginning to get used to this. Everything that I did with Dexter had to do with teaching and learning. We did nothing without him using even the most simplest things to teach me.

That same night after we'd finished eating Dexter said he needed to go by a grocery store and pick up something. Birdie left to go meet one of her daughters and Dexter and I went to the grocery store.

Dexter said, "What I need is some bottled water and I also need some licorice."

I didn't realize at that time, but Dexter loved licorice. He especially loved black licorice. That was his favorite kind.

We found the licorice and bottled water and some other things and even in the grocery store Dexter continued teaching me.

He would say, "Ron why do you think that this isle has this particular display?"

I would say, "Well Dexter, I really don't know."

He'd say, "Don't you think it's because the display gets your attention for this particular item in this way?"

He would explain to me the psychology behind the placement of the items on the grocery shelf.

At one point I stopped him and asked, "Dexter have you been to school to study this?"

He said, "No. You know me Ron. I only graduated from high school. I had a scholarship opportunity to go to Yale University through a relative of mine but I wanted to own my own business. I want to have my own opportunity to develop my own income. So I didn't go to the university or get a college degree. You know that."

Well then how," I said, "in the world do you know all this? How do you figure this out?"

He said, "I don't know. I just think about it. I try to observe things. I always ask myself the question, 'Why is this the way it is?' 'Why did this store organize in this way?' 'What is the owner of this store trying to do?' When I'm in this particular store, or another like it, I'm always asking myself, 'Why do people seem to go in on the left?' 'Why do people buy more things from the frozen food area than from the one behind it?' I'm always trying to watch and learn."

"No," he said, "I've never had any formal study of this. I just watch and learn and listen and I think. I always pray for God to help me understand things."

Dexter smiled at this point and said, "It's pretty exciting! Isn't it? There's always something new to learn."

I believe this was part of the reason for Dexter's exuberant, youthful spirit. However a man older than me with grandchildren, and yet his vitality overflowed continually. His excitement and love of life impressed everyone around him. He was always learning. He was always hungry to grow.

When we finished at the grocery store we went out to his pickup truck. This was Dexter's new truck and he wanted to drive it rather than the Mercedes. When I got in the truck and sat down I heard a loud crunching sound underneath me like something cracking, or breaking. Startled, I reached underneath myself and pulled out a cassette tape holder. The tape inside was alright, but the holder was cracked. I'd sat down hard on it and cracked it.

This was long before CD's and DVD's. The technology had not quite advanced into those areas yet. Dexter used cassette tapes for giving out his teaching. This was a tape by another man that he was listening to.

When I picked it up and showed him I said, "Dexter I'm so sorry. The tape is alright, but I broke the case."

He said, "That's alright Ron. Who have you got there?"

I looked at it. If I remember correctly it was a friend of Dexter's named Jerry Meadows. I told Dex it was a tape by Jerry and then said, "You know that's the first person who introduced me to you in Huntsville, Alabama."

Dexter ginned and said, "Oh yes. Now you listen to his tapes don't you?"

I said, "Well Dexter, as a matter-of-fact yes, because I found Jerry to be an outstanding and insightful speaker."

Dexter said, "Well look at this."

He reached underneath the seat of his new truck and pulled out a box filled with cassette tapes. He said, "These are friends of mine. These are business leaders. Ron all of them have something important to say. I'll pick a few of them and I listen to some of this tape and some of that tape."

As he was explaining this to me I thought, "WOW. If a man like Dexter Yager, who already knows so much and is at the peak of his own learning curve, needs to grow and he needs to listen to tapes and he needs to gather new information, then so do I. So does everyone else.

It fit what Dexter was teaching me that visit. Keep growing. That's what Dexter kept telling me. Keep growing. That's what I was beginning to experience as I looked at all the cassette tapes in the car.

I still had my 67 questions. I'd already gone through a number of them. In fact I'd gone through 43 of them and had a few yet to go.

I remember saying, "Dexter we have done 43 questions. Can we do some more?"

He said, "That's great. Let's go ahead and do it."

So we drove around in the truck for another two hours as I advanced questions to Dexter and he gave me thoughtful and insightful answers. This went on until 2 o'clock in the morning.

Dexter said, "You know, let's go get something to drink."

We went to a convenience store and got bottles of water.

When we came back out Dexter said, "How many questions do you have left?"

I had four questions remaining. We went through those four4 questions and Dexter answered them. I thought, "This is great. I've done another list. This is amazing! This was close to 300 questions in a four month period. I was so hungry to grow myself that I wanted to pick his brain and know everything I could about everything I could think to ask.

After I finished the 4th question it was 3:30 in the morning. We were still driving around in the pickup truck and Dexter began to explain something to me. He was talking about something connected with financial decision making and how to avoid being manipulated by other people, but still love those people. He explained how you never want to make a needless enemy.

I heard those words, but somehow they became blurred in my mind. It seemed as if Dexter was becoming distant from me. I was aware of exiting backwards through a long, dark tunnel. Then in my mind I could see Amy and other people around me who were walking on the beach and talking and laughing and having a great time. After a few moments something jarred like an earthquake on the beach. Something jolted me. My eyes flew open and I then realized that I had fallen asleep while Dexter was still speaking. It was 4 o'clock in the morning on the clock on the dash of the pickup truck. I was actually leaning forward and the only thing that was holding me in place was the straps of the seatbelt. If you had undone the seatbelt I would have fallen onto the dash of the truck. I was that far gone.

To this day I do not know if Dexter was aware that I was asleep. When I came to and left the "mental" beach that I'd been dreaming about Dexter was still teaching me about finances and telling me what I needed to learn and know. I shook off my drowsiness and realized that I'd fallen asleep so easily. I didn't want that to happen again and I was embarrassed and wondered if Dexter would be upset if he knew.

I glanced over and saw a grin on his face and a twinkle in his eye. I remember thinking maybe he did know after all. I'm still not sure to this day. If he did know it he never condemned me or ridiculed me. He just kept talking. I woke up and we proceeded from there.

At 4:45 that morning we drove back to the lake house on Lake Wylie. We got out of the car and noticed Birdie's car was already there. Dexter and I drove into his garage and put the truck away.

I looked at my watch and saw it was just a few minutes after 5 o'clock. I remember thinking, " Here is comes! Another dawn with Dexter."

But I'd noticed something. By the time we had gone through all these questions I noticed that when we came to the 3 and 4 and 5 and 6 o'clock morning hours there was a special bond; a closeness; a comfortable connection that did not exist during any other time of the visits that he and I had together. These early morning hours were so special in themselves. Not just the quiet and tranquility of the night hours, but for some reason there was an openness that I began to have during those hours that did not match my openness at any other time.

It was not a choice. It was not that I didn't want to have openness at other times. I just didn't have it. During these early morning hours as the dawn began to approach I realized that Dexter was bringing both of us to a place where my ability to learn was enhanced by all the hours we had spent together. Now as we shared the beauty of the dawn of the new day there was a dimension of learning and development that was unlike anything else I'd ever experienced in my life.

We sat there for a few more minutes. I knew that there was more that I was going to experience in the next hour before the sun really came up. I sat there; the sleepiness and drowsiness all gone with every sense alert to what Dexter was teaching me.

It reminds me of another experience I had with Dexter some years after these first early dawns. Dexter and I were traveling in Europe together. Birdie and Amy had gone shopping and were spending the night in Frankfort, Germany. Dexter and two friends of his and myself all went to a suit factory in a small village to be measured for some custom made clothing.

Dexter had made all the arrangements. We had finished some extraordinary effective Christian rallies that were not related to his business, but rallies that presented Jesus Christ to people in that part of Germany. The response had been gigantic and we were all tired, but happy with what we had seen God accomplish during those rallies.

The four of us piled into a small motor home and drove to the village where the suit factory was located. We had finished the last rally the night before.

Dexter said, "Why don't we go so that we are the first people to be at the doors at the suit factory at 8:00 in the morning?"

We all thought that was a great idea. We were wired up anyway. We drove for several hours in the darkness of the German night through small, tiny villages on narrow roadways. We finally arrived at the village where the suit factory was located.

By this time it was 4:00 in the morning and we needed to wait four more hours to be the first people there when the doors opened. Dexter had already explained to us how important it was for us to be first because this was a very busy factory. People come from all over Europe and different parts of the world. He didn't want us to get there too late and there be many people ahead of us so we would have to spend our whole day there. If we were there early we could be "in and out" and go back and pick up Birdie and Amy and go on with the rest of our tour.

Here it was 4:00 in the morning and I realized here was another dawn with Dexter! After we ate a few bites of whatever was available in the motor home it was after 4:30 and all of us were beginning to doze off.

Suddenly Dexter stood up in the motor home and he said, "Wait a minute. Does anybody have an alarm clock?"

I looked and my bags were with Amy back at the hotel so I had nothing. We discovered no one else had an alarm clock either. There was not an alarm clock in the whole motor home.

Dexter then announced, "Our goal and purpose is to be at that suit factory when the doors open at 8:00. Alright. Nobody sleeps. NOBODY SLEEPS!"

We said, "Dexter! No! We are so tired."

He said, "Nope. Our purpose; our mission; our goal; our reason for being here is to be there when they open at 8:00. If we're going to pick up Amy and Birdie on time, then we have to keep this schedule. If we're going to keep our commitments to everybody else then we need to keep that schedule. NOBODY SLEEPS!"

Every time one of us would start to go to sleep Dexter would throw water on us. We complained and begged, "Oh no. Please no more." He would laugh and throw more water on us.

Finally around 7:15 in the morning we cleaned up as best we could. We weren't a very pretty sight. We didn't look good. We didn't smell good.

We didn't feel good. But, we were awake!

We went out to a small village store and bought brown German bread, German sausages, home-cured cheese and bottles of Coke Cola. We all consumed everything we could. It was one of the best breakfasts I've had in my life!

We were still groggy, but at 8 o'clock when that factory opened, we were the first in line. Dexter ushered us in. Different staff members welcomed us because they had seen Dexter before. They all remembered his friendliness and good natured camaraderie and how he related to everyone. People loved Dexter!

Dexter had said, "This is going to be great for everybody because it's not expensive." He was right. It was very inexpensive. But the quality was exceptional.

The four of us spent almost two hours picking out swatches of clothing and deciding on designs we wanted. By this time we all had gotten something of a second wind. We kept drinking coffee and Cokes for the caffeine so we could keep going.

We arrived back in Frankfort late that afternoon to pick up Birdie and Amy. We had dinner with them and then drove to Luxembourg. By then we were more than ready to sleep. We crashed as quickly as we could. We were all wiped out.

I will never forget that particular dawn with Dexter because it revealed his commitment to his goals. It revealed his self discipline. It revealed his determination to fulfill a goal once he had made it.

Of course I didn't know all the events of that story in Germany when I was sitting with Dexter on Lake Wylie that morning. However, that experience in Germany is very consistent with all that I'd been learning.

Even in the early morning hours Dexter never lost his focus. He never lost his purpose. He never lost his sense of mission.

I realize now that Dexter sees himself as a man of destiny. I don't mean he thinks he is better than others or proud or arrogant in any way. That's not what he feels. He sees himself as a man with God's purpose on his life. That purpose involves helping and blessing and developing and mentoring other people.

Whether it was in Germany saying, "NOBODY SLEEPS! Our goal is to be at the suit factory."; Or whether it's with me at 6:00 in the morning at this latest dawn with Dexter saying, "Ron do you have anymore questions?"—Dex wanted to squeeze every moment of value out of this time together.

He asked, "Do you have anything else at all that you can personally think of?"

This was Dexter through and through. A man who never lost his focus. Never lost sight of his purpose. Never lost sight of the particular goal that he was going for at that time. On this morning that I've been describing, we finally saw the full dawn. I was beginning to slow down. Dexter had slept later than normal the night before so he was still going strong at 7:45 in the morning.

Finally at 8:30 I said, "Dexter I have to leave at noon. I had better sleep."

Dexter said, "I don't want you to get hurt. Listen Ron, these times are so special and so valuable and so important but you tell me if ever you think you need to sleep. This will be a bargain between us. If you need to sleep or go to bed you tell me."

Of course my thought even while he's saying this was, "Go to sleep? Go to bed? I don't want to miss a word of this! I don't want to miss a second of this!"

I smiled and thanked him and said, "Dexter that's great. Thank you. I may take you up on that if I need to."

At 8:30 I ate a high fiber oatmeal raisin cookie with Dexter and we stood together as the sunlight glistened on the waters of Lake Wylie and the dawn broke everywhere. We prayed together. We prayed for God to anoint one another.

The word anoint means for God to give special favor and power to someone. It's a special consideration from God himself onto your life. That's what we always would pray for one another.

I prayed that morning, "Lord anoint Dexter. Give him special power to do what you've called him to do."

Dexter then prayed for me, "Lord anoint Ron and give him special power to do what You've called him to do."

Then we would pray for one another's safety and one another's family members. We always ended in the name of Jesus, our common, mutual Savior.

After the prayer that morning I went to the guest bedroom and collapsed on the bed. Sometimes I would hear Dexter still walking around. Sometimes I would notice the phone light on my phone by the bed coming on, indicating that Dexter was talking to someone. Usually Dexter was still going, even when I was wiped out.

Gradually I drifted off to sleep. I had my small alarm clock with me and it went off at noon. I got up and took a quick shower and headed home.

Amy was waiting for me. "What happened?" she asked. "What did he teach you this time?"

I pulled out all my notes and said, "You gotta hear this! This has been amazing. You gotta hear this." I was experiencing an education of a type and manner that I had never thought possible. I was learning from a great man who had done great things. Dexter was willing to take a not so great person—me—and was willing to help make me a better man for God.

That was my latest dawn with Dexter.

CHAPTER 6
Love In Action

D exter Yager loves people. I had realized that early on. He doesn't use people. He doesn't manipulate people. He really likes them and really cares for them. I believe that part of that arises from his commitment to Jesus Christ, because Jesus loves people. The Bible teaches that Jesus Christ, through the Holy Spirit lives within each person's heart who knows Christ. Because Jesus loves people that is a primary and wonderful element to Christian living in general. Dexter shows that.

I have always been fascinated with how Dexter relates to people. I know individuals who say they love people, and I think they really do, but they are awkward and uncomfortable around them. They don't know how to talk to certain individuals so they create a wall between them and another person. It's what I call "living in the bubble." I see people who walk up and down city streets and they are so pre-occupied by their own situations and their own concerns and their own worries and their own thoughts that they never connect with another person. They will spend the whole day inside their own private bubble walking from place to place and only interacting with someone so they can get something or purchase something or take care of a work requirement. Generally they avoid personal contact with other human beings.

Dexter Yager has never been like that. He seeks out people. The more difficult the person, the more awkward the situation, the more he loves to jump into it. If we're in a situation together and he meets someone who doesn't want to talk Dexter is highly challenged. He

97

likes to bring that person out and create a human connection with them.

I remember one occasion when we were driving around one night and stopped at the security gates of a large development on a lake. Dexter, as usual, was showing me property. We got out of the car and a man walked over and rudely accosted us and demanded we leave. He said we had no business being there.

Dexter said, "I own property here and I have a security pass to come in."

The man said, "Oh yes. Of course you do. Sure you do. Where is it?"

Dexter could not produce the security document. He didn't have it with him. But said, "I'm sure that you have some way to check and determine that I'm one of the owners inside the development."

The man said, "No, you just get on your way."

About this time a pickup truck drove up. The lights were on as it was twilight. A man got out of the truck and saw what was happening and hurried over.

He said, "Dexter! Are you here to see some more of your properties? It doesn't matter what time it is. I'm sure we can get you in."

At this moment it was obvious that the man coming out of the pickup truck was the boss and the security guard that had so rudely talked to us was his employee. You can imagine the reaction that the employee had to the boss. He realized that he had made a major blunder. He had committed a public relations mistake. He had insulted in front of another man, meaning me, an individual who was a major owner within this development. Also his boss, on top of everything, knew this man Dexter Yager. I'm sure that this man who had been so impolite and discourteous expected that Dexter would take the boss aside and relay to him what had happened and demand that the man be fired.

I stood there for a moment wondering what Dexter would do. To my surprise, and I'm sure the immense relief of the security guard, Dexter walked over to the boss and said, "Why Charlie I'm so glad to see you too. Yep, I brought my friend Ron and we're going to go in and look around if that's ok."

Then he walked over and put his arm around the security guard who had been so impolite and he said, "Charlie this new guy is really on the money. He checks everybody out and he's going to protect this place. This guy was really doing his job. He was making sure that nobody got in without the right security pass and I appreciate that because I've got property here myself."

The look on the man's face was a revelation. At that moment the man had made a decision that from this point on if he had an opportunity to do anything for Dexter Yager he was going to do it. Dexter made a friend for life with that moment of reassurance and commendation. Dexter made no reference to the man's rudeness or comment on his discourtesy. He said nothing about him not believing us when Dexter had said he had security clearance to go in. Dexter only commended the man for "doing his job."

Dexter showed me that night that he's not vindictive. He always tries to find a way to win the person over. He doesn't do it through compromise or saying things that are not true. He does it in a way that the person knows that "this man believes in me."

I was in a great Free Enterprise celebration in Charlotte, North Carolina. There were over 25,000 people packed into this coliseum. While I was walking down one of the back area corridors beneath the coliseum Dexter came around a corner. I was walking with my mother and father who had come to hear me speak that night.

Dexter walked over and saw my mom and dad and warmly greeted them. After a few moments of conversation Dexter put his arm around me and looked at my mother and my father and said, "You know we love Ron. All of us know that there's a great man in there trying to get out. We're going to help that man come out and be as great as he can be." My mom beamed and my dad was proud. Dexter chatted another moment and then went down the hall to his responsibilities.

That's what I mean when I say Dexter loves people. He didn't need to spend all these dawns with me, an unknown pastor. He didn't need to take his valuable days and nights and invest them in me. He committed on his own and gave himself freely, unstintingly to help a young man to develop in ways that I don't think could have been possible otherwise.

Once when I was with Dexter in a meeting in his home I watched him manage egos. This was a meeting of good men; Christian men. They were all high powered successful individuals. Each one owned his own business and each one was accustomed to being in charge. I watched Dexter treat them with great respect. As an observer, I watched him manage their concerns in such a way that no one was uncomfortable or insulted.

At one particular point in the meeting one leader spoke up and was aggravated about something that had occurred in a previous convention. Dexter calmed him and listened to him with great respect and said, "We have to deal with that. You're concerns are why we're here. I want to know what you think."

This man who had started with the heat of emotion began to visibly calm. He and Dexter then discussed what needed to be done to correct the situation. The man seemed proud that Dexter had respected his opinion and cared for his input.

Throughout that meeting I watched as Dexter listened and commented. At times he would stop and pray for someone right in the middle of the meeting. Remember that Dexter is an unconventional personality. He has his own way of doing things. This may jar and startle some people but to Dexter it is just being himself. These are genuine Dexter moments.

One of those moments came when he stopped the meeting to pray. He didn't pray the way you would expect someone to pray. There was no formality or religious lingo or any sanctimonious seminary vocabulary.

We were sitting in a room with all six of these men and myself discussing very sensitive subjects. I was privileged just to be there and had already expressed my commitment to keep my mouth shut about everything that was said. I was going to respect my opportunity to be there. In the middle of this meeting someone mentioned that someone in their business group had cancer and was very ill.

Dexter said, "We've got to pray for them!"

Here we were discussing matters of tremendous financial significance to these men involving tens of millions of dollars and Dexter says, "We've got to pray for this man!"

Did Dexter have us stand around and hold hands and bow our heads? No he didn't. The very next thing that Dexter did after having said we need to pray for this man was start talking to God. His eyes were wide open in front of everybody as if God were sitting right there in the room with us, which of course He was!

Dexter naturally began to talk to God and said, "Lord we need Your help with this. In the name of Jesus touch this man and heal him. You know that he needs Your help right now and his friends here have brought this up to us. Lord we need you to do this right now in Jesus' name. Where two or more are gathered together in Jesus' name, You promise it shall be done. Lord we believe You."

In the very next breathe, without even an "Amen," Dex looked around and said, "Alright, what's the next order of business?"

Dexter was always doing things like that. Talking to God was as natural to Dex as talking with any other person in the room. When a need was brought up Dexter always stopped us to pray for it. It wasn't in just that situation, it happened all the time. Whenever we were with anyone and someone said "Dexter this is a person in need. This is a person in trouble." Dexter would immediately pray for them and ask God in the name of Jesus to touch them; to help them; to heal them; to provide for them in whatever way was needed.

What was so remarkable to me was that weeks later I would be back with Dexter and I would ask him, "Do you ever wonder whatever happened to such-and-such a person who we prayed for?" Dexter would say, "Oh I've already followed that up." In all the cases I remember he would have checked on the person and found out information. He remembered each individual.

When I say that Dexter loves people I mean it. I have witnessed it. I have experienced it. It is so genuine and so real for him. Here is a man for whom giving is a way of life and loving is the language of his heart.

I've been describing this particular meeting where we stopped to pray for the individual and people were discussing all their financial matters and questions related to a convention that Dexter was sponsoring involving tens of thousands of people all over the world. At the end of that meeting on that particular day I was going to be with him for part of the day and he was going to be with these men for the rest of the day. The schedule had been worked out in that manner.

I recall that when I had gone home the next day that I had been so affected by this kind of leadership that I prayed the whole way home asking God to make me like that. I arrived at my house in Kentucky. No one was home. Amy and Allison were gone. I went into the house and walked into the bathroom.

At that time, Amy had a woman who was helping her with house work one day a week and assisting her with cleaning projects. This lady would come about three hours once a week and help Amy. That particular day she had worked in the morning and I then had arrived in the afternoon to find no one home.

When I walked into the bathroom I saw to my horror that something terrible had happened! The toilet paper was dropping from the bottom and I preferred it over the top. The woman helping Amy had put the new roll of toilet paper on in a way that I didn't like.

I remember standing there and becoming angry and irritated thinking, "What is wrong with this woman? I have told her how I like certain things done. What is wrong with her?

I started to feel my anger mount and my negative emotion increase. Just as I turned to walk out of the bathroom I ran face-to-face into Dexter. No, he wasn't really there, but he was there in my heart and my mind and in my imagination and his example was there.

When I say that I ran into Dexter I didn't physically, literally do that, but I ran into what I'd been learning from him. It was as if he were standing there and looking at me saying, "Ron, you don't know what that woman goes through. You don't know what that woman puts up with. You don't know how hard she works to help people clean houses. You're a Christian and you're angry with her over the positioning of a toilet paper roll? My, my Ron you must not have learned anything yet."

Dexter's example at that moment softened my heart. I prayed for God to forgive me.

Once I was in a meeting sponsored by one of Dex's Diamond leaders. I was very tired as I had just returned with my family from Australia and New Zealand. We were in Florida at the Orlando Convention Center. Early one morning I went to run for several miles.

When I came back I went past my room by mistake. I realized in my haste that I had passed by the door. I went back and was irritated for a moment because I thought that I'd left early enough that the maid would have finished cleaning the room. But she was still there. She was going more slowly than I liked and taking her time. I wanted to go take a shower and get ready and get out of there. I was getting irritated. I almost said something to her because she didn't see me in the doorway. I almost said to her, "Why can't you hurry?"

Then with her back to me and without ever seeing me this young Hispanic woman, in somewhat broken English, began to softly sing "Jesus loves me, this I know. For the Bible tells me so."

I was thankful that Dexter's example was always a protective mechanism in my heart, in my life, in my relationships with other people. In my shame I slipped out the door and prayed, "God forgive me. Help me be more like Dexter. Help me be more like You."

On one occasion Dexter and I were at the Atlanta Hilton Hotel. Birdie and Amy were also there because Dexter was there to receive an award. I was hosting him. This event involved the National Christian Booksellers Association. Dexter was a guest and I was a guest. We were having a great time staying at the Hilton and going to the convention the next day.

Dexter and I stayed up until dawn. We weren't suppose to be at the convention until late in the afternoon the next day so Dexter was on his customary schedule.

At 4 o'clock in the morning Dexter wanted something to eat. Birdie and Amy were already asleep in their rooms so he and I went to the Atlanta Hilton's small casual coffee shop that stays open all night. We were the only ones there. A waitress came over and asked us what we wanted. We ordered breakfast and then began to chat with the waitress.

Dexter took about 15 minutes and did what he always did. I've seen Dexter do this hundreds of times. He forgot about the food. He ignored every other consideration and just zeroed in on this waitress.

After a few minutes she was sitting beside us and Dexter looked at her and said, "What are your dreams? What do you want out of life? What motivates you the most? What excites you the most? What do you want the most?"

The woman, who we'd only met minutes before, began to pour her heart and soul out to us. She was a single mom and struggling. Her husband had abandoned her and walked out with another woman. She was now trying to work multiple jobs. She would drive 50 miles one way to this little all night restaurant and then drive 50 miles back so that she could earn enough to send her children to a private Christian school. Dexter pulled her out and she relayed all this personal information.

Dexter then said, "Here's what I want you to do. There is somebody in your area to help you start a business. I'm going to put you in touch with him."

She gave him an address and phone number. She completely trusted him even though we were total strangers.

Dexter then said, "Now sweetheart…"

Dexter was old enough and grandfatherly enough that he could get away with calling her sweetheart. But he said, "Now sweetheart we're going to pray for you."

So he began to pray for her and pray for God to help her and to protect her children. This woman sat there and cried. We were the only ones there at 5 o'clock in the morning. This woman sat there and cried and cried.

By this time we were all on a first name basis and she said, "Thank you Dexter. We'll keep in touch."

She did! She actually did! Sometime later Dexter gave me follow-up information about her. He didn't forget her. He didn't forget anybody that we ever talked to in all those years of our relationship. He doesn't to this day.

I was with Dexter recently and he did this with a server in a restaurant who no one knew at the table. But Dexter became her buddy; her pal; her friend within a matter of minutes. I've seen him do this at a gym that he works out in. I'll see Dexter again in a few weeks and I know he'll do it again. Why? Because he never fails in his desire to touch the hearts and lives of other people. He never fails in his hunger to be God's instrument to change another man or woman for good.

It doesn't matter that these people are strangers. It doesn't matter that these individuals are people that he doesn't know. None of that makes any difference because here is Dexter's people connection.

I remember once when I arrived at Dexter's for one of my dawn meetings. I was a bit late. Dexter asked me if I could exit the house for a short time because he had another couple there whom he needed to speak to for awhile.

I left and came back about four hours later. I knew that Dexter would not use my time unless it was very important. He is, and always has been extremely sensitive as to another person's schedule. He's always considerate of my schedule. I had no problem leaving for those four hours because I trusted his judgment.

When I came back to the house the couple that he'd been speaking to had already left. Dexter asked me if I knew who had just been there.

I said, "No."

He said, "Well, this is in total confidence. Don't ever reveal this or talk about this."

He then told me who the couple was. This couple is known in some circles all over the country. They are a well known Christian leadership couple. Dexter had spent four hours with them in marriage counseling. No one who saw them publicly would have suspected that there was even a hint of a problem. They had sought out Dexter Yager on this dark night at his lake house to see if he would help them with marriage counseling.

He said, "Ron you know the interesting thing about them? I've known them for several years and spent some time with them in the past. They've been on television and been in different Christian leadership circles."

He said, "When they asked to see me I knew that it must be important. I could tell it was important by the way they asked. I could tell it was important by looking at them when they arrived. Even though this couple have a commitment to Jesus Christ and they want God to use them they have a certain form of pride that had created a barrier. You could sense it from the very opening of the conversation.

"She wanted help. He wanted help. However neither would admit where each one might be wrong. Ron we were together for four hours. It literally took three of those hours for them just to be honest with me."

I asked Dex if that tired him or effected him.

He said, "Ron this one was exhausting. Not only was there the intensity of their emotions toward one another, but also there was my awareness of how this couple is respected and loved by so many thousands of people. I knew that I needed God's unusual help to help me help them. Yes, it was exhausting."

I asked him what it was like with other people. Now understand, this was late into the night. The couple had already left. He'd been with them for four hours and it was now around midnight.

Dexter answered, "I can't think about getting tired. I can't think about wearing out because these people need me."

You might think that Dexter is elevating his own importance, but this is not true at all. I knew that his attitude of generosity was so genuine and there was no personal selfishness mixed in it that I could detect. He just wanted this couple to be helped.

I then said, "Dexter if it became known that you were the instrument to help this well known Christian leadership couple...why people all over the country would be grateful to you."

Dexter said, "No Ron no. No one must ever know this story. No one must ever know that they were here. That would embarrass them. They are working out their marriage problems. They're going to be okay. They're going to stay together. They do love each other. Their going to stick it out and are going to be okay.

"What if it were known that they were here for this kind of counseling? That would hang over them. People would then look at them and wonder if anything else was wrong. It would create a suspicion that this couple possibly had other things wrong with them.

"You know what I want to do? I want to protect their reputation. I want to protect their commitment to one another so that no one ever even suspects there ever having been a problem."

I realized that Dexter could have flaunted his role in this situation, but he refused to do so. Do you know why? Because it would not have helped the couple. His whole purpose was to help them and their marriage. He didn't seek any credit. He didn't seek any consideration or praise. He just did it and God blessed him and God used him.

This is what I believe to be a window into Dexter's heart. Dexter is not perfect. In fact in a later chapter I'm going to deal with Dexter's failures and the things that have disappointed him in his life. I'm very candid in that chapter about things he's told me that he's had to struggle with and overcome. I believe as far as Dexter's basic motivation for helping people that it is totally and entirely real.

Let me tell you something else. That was a special night. That particular night something happened that gave me an even deeper insight into Dexter Yager. We did some of our usual things. It was by this time almost 1 o'clock in the morning. We went to the all night Denny's where everybody knew Dexter. Dexter spent about ½ hour talking to the guests and the cooks and everybody who was in there. He was loving them and connecting with them.

We next drove around for another hour until about 2:30 in the morning. Everything was right on schedule. We were doing the things that we usually did. You might wonder how we did property examination in the middle of the night when it was so dark. Dexter would carry large flashlights. These were the long police flashlights. I've mentioned them before. Dexter used them to put spotlights on properties. At one time he had a vehicle that had a large spotlight mounted on his car. He had it installed so he'd have a huge beam to see property with.

This night was no exception. We ate at the Denny's. We greeted everyone. We looked at all the properties. All the while Dexter was teaching me.

I noticed on this particular night that Dexter seemed a bit tired. It was probably because he'd had the four hours of intense counseling with the couple who had needed help and needed a break through. Dexter was aware that this couple was important and he didn't want to fail them.

Dexter had given quite a bit of himself that night, but he didn't give any hint to me that he was wanting to cut my time short. He didn't give any indication that he wanted me to leave early or not do my questions. Instead he tried even harder to answer the questions that I had brought him.

Yes I did have questions this night, but only 46 questions. I was running a bit low because I'd asked so many already. I tried to make sure that the 46 questions I did have were thoughtful and had particular meaning to them and the answer to those questions would matter. I tried to come up with questions that would be important enough to take up Dexter's time.

At 3 o'clock in the morning even Dexter was tired. We drove back to the lake house. We went in and discovered Birdie had slept for a couple of hours and was now up again. Birdie was sifting through some mail and looking at packages that had been delivered. She also was reading some messages from her children.

Dexter excused himself and spent some time with Birdie so they could catch up on the day. He was very thoughtful to her. The two of them were away for about 45 minutes. I waited and walked around and spent time thinking and praying and going through the remainder of my questions. I only had seven questions left of my 46 questions for that night. I reviewed the seven I had left and was reorganizing them and preparing for Dexter's return.

I was sitting in a small office that Birdie had for her concerns and needs. While I was there the phone began to ring. Dexter came in and answered it and talked to someone for a few minutes and then hung up.

Then Dexter said, "Let me check my voice mail. Do you mind Ron?"

I said, "No that's fine."

Dexter went into his voice mail. After a few minutes I could see by the look on his face that something was not quite right. Dexter listened very carefully and then he dictated into the voice mail a very specific answer to an awkward question.

I found out later what happened. I'll bring you in on it. This is the background on what occurred.

Dexter has a private voice mail with an unlisted number. Only a few people have that number. On this particular night someone had called Dexter's voice mail and had addressed Dexter by name. However Dexter did not know how this person had gotten his voice mail number. It was someone he did not know. It was a person who was angry with Dexter and was accusing him of interfering in her life.

It happened that Dexter had recently made a speech where he referenced the subject of abortion. He had expressed the clear Christian position that abortion is wrong. I agreed with Dexter on that. That is the Biblical position.

Dexter had not expressed his position in an offensive way. I was present in the meeting the woman had attended. I remember him saying that he cared about women who had gone through an abortion but believed that it had become too easy to get one. He went on to say that he believed we were cheapening human life and he did express a very clear and definite position on the subject.

This woman had heard him speak in the convention and somehow had gotten his voice mail number. She blistered him on the phone. In fact he played the message for me. She was angry and yelling into the phone. She was calling him names and told him he had no right to say these things. Dexter saved her message and motioned for me to come over.

He said, "Ron we need to pray for this woman and then I'm going to call her back."

I said, "Dex you don't have too. She's a total stranger."

He said, "Nope. I'm going to call her back. That woman is so angry and has said these hateful things to me because she's hurt. There's some reason she's hurt and we gotta figure out what it is and help her. We have to do that."

We stopped and prayed for this woman. We didn't know her name as she had not given it on the message. We prayed and asked God to help her and to comfort her and to meet her need and to calm her spirit and to speak to her heart.

Dexter then looked at me and gave a smile and the twinkle was back in his eye. He loves a challenge. He pushed the answer button and answered her message back to her voice mail.

For the next few minutes I listened as Dexter explained his thinking on abortion and explained the Biblical position. He did this in a very loving and thoughtful and gentle way.

Then he said, "I want to thank you for calling me. I want to thank you for being nice enough to tell me all this."

When he said that I remember thinking, "She was not nice at all!"

Dexter continued his message and said, "I want to thank you for giving me this information. I want you to know that I have a friend here who is a pastor. We have prayed for you. If I can help you or do anything for you at all I want to do it. God bless you and you have my prayers. Thank you again for being nice enough to get in touch with me."

He said all this in the most loving sweet message. He could have easily hit the delete button. He could have easily said he had some jerk on the phone whose gotten his number and was trying to embarrass him. He did none of that. In fact, he didn't even take it personally.

I found out later that Dexter does get hurt. He gets hurt a lot. He feels that hurt. He's not a robot. He's not an automaton with no feelings. He's not a machine that operates with no emotion. He is very real. He is very human and when you cut him he bleeds. When you hurt him he hurts.

I'm sure that this woman hurt him that night. I listened to her message and she said spiteful and hateful and distasteful things to him. She called him unpleasant names that were not appropriate.

Yet his one concern before he called her back was, "Why is she so hurt? Why is she feeling so abandoned? Ron I don't want to do anything to keep her from Jesus Christ. I don't want to do anything to keep her from the Lord. I know that she's mad and I know that she's upset. But I want to make sure that I leave her with a good feeling in her heart toward God and toward me as much as I can."

That's when we prayed and that's when Dex gave her the answer that he gave her. This was very special for me to see how Dexter handled this situation.

I had heard Dexter on other occasions speak to people who were upset with him about a particular position that he expressed or something that he had said or something that he communicated. Each and every time he was thoughtful and considerate to the person who was upset with him.

Here he was in the middle of the night. He was tired. He had given specific counsel to the couple that had come to his home. On top of that he had spent hours and hours with me. I know that he was tired. I know that he was at the limit of his own physical resources. I could tell this was the most tired that I had ever seen him on any of our nights or dawns together. Yet he spent extra time reassuring and loving this woman who had been so hateful and so spiteful with him.

This is not to say that Dexter was or is perfect. I'm not saying that there has never been a time when Dexter has not done the right thing. What I'm saying is at this time of 4 o'clock in the morning, with this person giving him this kind of abuse, this was the real Dexter. He had every reason in the world not to answer her. How did she even get his private voice mail number? She had no business having his private voice mail. But I watched and saw that he didn't even concern himself with that. He just tried to help the woman and comfort her and pray for her.

By this time it was almost 5 o'clock in the morning. The faint glimmer of the sun was just beginning to come up over the lake. It was to be another dawn with Dexter.

Dexter said, "Ron if you need to you can go to bed a little earlier tonight."

I knew what he was really saying. Dex wanted to go to bed early, but he was giving me the option to choose. He told me once that since I made the effort to come to his house and used my time and expense to come and be with him he wanted to honor that. He wanted to give me the maximum benefit possible for our time together.

Remember I still had seven questions to go. I decided to not even mention them. I could always keep them for the next visit.

I answered him, "Dexter let's just forget it. No problem. I think I am a little tired. I think I could go to bed as well."

He smiled and said, "Let's have a cookie and go to bed."

We went into the kitchen and had an enormous oatmeal raisin high fiber cookie. These cookies were bigger than my hand. They were almost like a hubcap of a small car. But they were great!

We both had a cookie and drank some water and said our prayer together. The prayer as always was so heart felt. At 5:30 in the morning, with the dawn just beginning to break, we headed for bed just a little earlier on this particular occasion.

As I lay in bed that morning I thought of all the people with whom I interacted. I thought of times I was occasionally irritated with someone for whatever reason. I remember as I drifted off to sleep praying, "Lord thank you for giving me the privilege to be with this man and learn from his example. Lord help me love people. Not just the way Dexter loves people, but help me love people the way You love people. Dexter is trying to love people the way You love them and that's what I want to do too. Lord help me in Jesus name." I drifted off to sleep.

The next day I got up and Dexter and Birdie were still asleep. I took my usual noon shower and quickly dressed and started for home. I marveled on the long drive how God had allowed me to have this kind of relationship and education in my heart and in my life.

I was thankful for my latest dawn with Dexter.

CHAPTER 7
Overcoming Failure

When I was 10 years old, my parents decided to move from our small Kentucky community to Huntington, West Virginia. My dad had gotten a new job. When I received the news I was distressed. I had lived in the same small-town all my life. I had been born and reared among the same people. I was a happy part of a large extended family. Aunts, uncles, and cousins made up for my being an only child. I had friends and playmates and was popular in school and happy with my life. The move to Huntington disrupted all that. For the next two years we adjusted to our new community.

It was tough at first. My first week at school the teacher would continually mock me as a country hick. My accent was decidedly Southern country, and I did sound like I had grown up in a remote region.

One day she had me stand in front of the whole class and asked me to read something aloud. I did that and then she turned to the class and said, "I just wanted the class to hear how an uneducated, dumb hick sounds." I was 10 years of age. That was many years ago, but I've never forgotten the humiliation and embarrassment of that moment. The class erupted into laughter, and I sat down in shame and confusion.

Through the course of that year, things did improve. My mother and father were very close to me and I to them. My dog was with me, which was an element of stability in an uncertain time. Through the course of the year I did begin to make friends. I tried out for and made the school basketball team. I began to enjoy my new situation. But I never gave up my desire to return home to Eastern Kentucky.

Although at that point in my life I did not have a personal relationship with Jesus Christ, I would still pray and ask God to let us go home. When the news arrived that my dad had gotten another job in our hometown, I was elated. I remember the move back with great joy.

Throughout the summer after our return, I tried to re-contact my old friends. To my surprise, they had formed new associations and no longer welcomed me into their groups. When school began, no one would spend time with me, or talk to me. I was again confused and lost. I decided I had to adjust once again. I obviously survived those early years of turmoil and disruption. They caused no lasting damage.

However the memory of that time is still vivid today. Because that was the time in my life when I first felt like a failure. To feel like a failure is to experience an internal break-down of confidence. Your world shrinks. Your sense of stability lessens. You have the idea that life may not be as predictable or trustworthy as you'd once thought.

On my next trip to see Dexter, I was thinking about failure. Not necessarily the failure of my childhood experiences, but failure in general. I wanted to know something. I wanted to know if Dexter had ever experienced failure. Had Dexter gone through hard times? Had he had to overcome adversity?

When I met Dexter, he was at the top of his game. Success was everywhere. He was loved; respected; financially secure and involved with numerous high powered, ambitious individuals. His homes and collection of cars were visible statements of his achievement.

I wondered if he had ever gone through depression and difficulty and discouragement. I wanted to know.

When I arrived at the lake house that afternoon, it was very quiet. I thought first that a mistake might have occurred and possibly I had arrived on the wrong day. The car that Dexter usually drove was not there. The grounds were quiet. There was only the soft lap of the lake water and the occasional twitter of a bird in-flight. I rang the doorbell, but there was no response. I knocked hard twice with the same results. This was before cell phones, and I had no way to call the house.

I decided to wait. It was a nice afternoon. The setting of the lake was, as usual, beautiful and relaxing. This was a great opportunity for me to unwind after my drive. I always carry at least two books with me and my Bible. So I had something to read and something to study. It looked like a good afternoon after all, although I still was uncertain as to Dex's schedule and where he was.

After about half an hour, the car drove up and I saw with relief that it was Dexter and Birdie. Dexter drove up and leaned out of the window waving with a sweep of his arm and yelled, "Hey Ron! I'll be right in. Sorry we're late."

I waited a few minutes until he had entered the garage and come upstairs to open the door. When I went in Dexter smiled and said, "I've been to the dentist, and it took a little longer than I had planed. But sometimes you just have to do those things. Are you ready for a great day?

I said, "Dex...yes! I'm ready."

So began the next day leading to the next dawn with Dexter.

Dexter next put his pack down. When I say pack I mean a bag, or satchel that he carried everywhere. It contained extra sunglasses, some medications, notebooks, various personal items, I'd never seen Dexter without it. Sometimes I would offer to carry the bag for him, but wherever we went the bag went. Whenever Dexter set the bag down I knew that he would be there for at least a few minutes. So I waited.

He came back in and said, "Ron, my visit was great, but I would rather be doing things with you. What have you got for me today?

I said, "Dexter I want to ask you about something unusual. I want to know what you think about failure."

Dexter laughed, a truly hearty laugh, and said, "Well Ron the last two days Birdie and I have been swimming in a sea of garbage. It's almost as if every unpleasant thing has come our way. Just in two days too."

He said, "But you know, I made a decision. I could swim in this stuff, and maybe even sink. Or I could skim on the surface and slide on top of it and rise above it. That's what you have to do when you're being pulled down by the muck of life."

I was relieved. I thought, "Dexter does know something about overcoming failure."

I plunged into the discussion and said, "Dexter tell me more."

He motioned with his head and I walked over to the corner of his kitchen.

He said, "What does this say?"

I looked up and saw a humorous plaque on the wall. It showed a man waist deep in a swamp. Everywhere there were alligators and the man was desperately hitting the alligators with a stick to drive them away. The caption underneath a picture said something like "When you're trying to drain the swamp sometimes you find that you're waist deep in alligators and you've got to do something about that.

Dexter smiled and said, "Ron, that's what life is like. Sometimes when you take on a project, or attempt to reach a goal, there are unexpected alligators that come at you. You have to know how to beat them off and to escape and continue your project. If you're going to drain the swamp you're going to have to get rid of the alligators. And you're always going to have alligators."

We each sat down on a chair. Dexter looked at me and said, "Ron, let me ask you question. Have you had anyone get mad at you? Have you had people become angry with you? Do you have enemies who try to hurt you?"

I said, "Well Dexter, of course, there are people who on occasion have disagreed with what I've said or expressed their displeasure with something I've said. But I don't think I have true enemies, at least that I know of."

Dexter continued and said, "Let me be more specific. Have you ever had a newspaper print a lie about you? Have you ever had a reporter say something to you that was noticeably untrue, and you knew this. Have you ever had someone deliberately try to derail the direction of your life?"

I said, "Dexter, I don't quite know what that means. Can you tell me some more?"

He said, "Ron on one occasion a television program decided to interview me. They arranged to come to my home with their crew of cameras. Before the show was scheduled to be taped I had a preparation session with the host. He was friendly and tried to put me at ease. He wanted me to be comfortable, but I was not sure whether he could be trusted. In this case, it wasn't too bad.

"However, when the final show came out there were some things that were said and done and edited in such a way that I knew that it was not the way I intended to be. You might have heard of that show. It's called 60 Minutes and Mike Wallace is the man who interviewed me.

"Mike was very gracious. I have to admit that he was more fair with me than I expected. But there were certain things communicated on the show that were not accurate and not presented in a way that I had presented them."

"As a result of that," he said, "there were some misunderstandings about me and my business. Now what do you think my reaction should have been? Anger? Bitterness? Displeasure? No, my reaction was to move on and to trust God. That's always been my policy and that's always been my commitment. Trust God and move on. So when I ask you if you had people say things about you that were not true, what I'm actually aiming at is experiences such as what I just described."

I said, "Dexter I've not really done enough in life to be noticed by that kind of person, or that kind of show."

He said, "Well someday you will be and you'll need to be prepared for how to handle that at that point."

I looked at Dexter and I said, "There's more to this, isn't there?

Dex said, "Let me give you some more information. Sometimes people accuse you of things, and you know in your heart they're not true. You know yourself. You know who you are. You know what kind of person you really are...inside...in the heart. Some people still decide to make it seem as if you are someone different. Someone who does not have good motivation.

He said with conviction, "You cannot let that cause you to react badly. You've asked me about failure. My experience with the television program and my experience with certain people who have disagreed with me, or disputed with me, might be seen as failure. Or, you could say it was just adversity or opposition. What people see as failure is often the normal ups and downs of life; the normal jealousies; the normal envy. I realized that because of the success God had blessed me with, that there were many people who took shots at me. There were many who threw criticism at me and decided to try to bring me down."

"Dexter I understand the idea of adversity and opposition and difficulty," I replied. "I understand those concepts. What I want to know is have you ever had real, personal failure?"

Dexter laughed again.

He answered, "Have I ever had real personal failure? Ron when I first started my business my excitement was so BIG. I saw this as a way to secure the financial future of my family. I wanted to make sure that their future was solidly taken care of. My business began to grow at first and my opportunity developed. I started to make money. All this was wonderful.

However, the first people that I had developed under me got out. The whole business fell apart. Just when I thought it was going to work they walked out, and I lost everything.

"Now what do you think my decision was at that point? Did I think the business must not work? No, I knew the business worked. I knew it was a business model that I believed in. It had worked for other people, it could still work for me.

"Did I think I'll never work with people again because these people had walked out on me? No, I decided that I would commit myself to a principal and I have followed that principal all my life. It's very simple. The principal is, if I lose one I'll find two to replace them. I will never be in bondage to the decisions of other people. I will never allow someone else deciding to quit to make me quit. If I lose one, I'll get two. If I lose two, I'll get four. If I lose four, I'll get eight. Ron there's always someone to replace the person who quit.

My business is a people business. It's an educational business. It's a motivational business. If I develop and love people and help them succeed, they will bless me in return. But I cannot ever quit based on what they do, or do not do. So yes, I do know about failure."

Dexter continued, "I've had failures in business. I've had failures financially. I've lost more money than most people have made. But I've made it back. I've made decisions that turned out to be wrong and I've made investments that did not payoff. I decided early though that no failure of performance, would keep me from pursuing my dreams. What I do is very simple. I had to learn to do this. I didn't do this naturally, or easily, because it's something that I had to learn. It's very simple. I learned every time there was a failure. Every time there was a disappointment I taught myself to move on and to not dwell on that thing.

I work with people, whose whole life has been poisoned by their failures and disappointments. They spend every conversation with me re-living the pain of the past. They cannot let it go. I hear the same stories again and again. I knew early in my life that I could not take in that kind of poison and live. I could not dwell on what did not work. If I lost the money in a deal or in an investments it was gone. I had to make more money to replace it. If someone quit my business, I was disappointed. Sometimes I was even hurt, because I always learn to love the people I work with. I care for every one of them. If they go though I cannot allow myself to dwell on their leaving. I have to trust in God and move forward. Move on, keep going.

I believe that a forward focus is critical to success. Now, you learn from your failures. You learn from the past. You learn from your disappointments, but you do not allow them to control your life, or your decisions, or your actions."

By this time it was almost five o'clock in the afternoon. Dexter had told me even more stories to support what he had been explaining to me about people who had hurt him and lied about him or disappointed him. I marveled at this man who showed no bitterness and no hatred or desire for revenge or thirst for vengeance. There was no effort to hurt anyone else, or slander another individual. He had truly gotten beyond those experiences.

During those two hours he told me about people I'd never met and names I'd never heard. I began to realize that if there were this many, Dexter must have experienced a number of disappointments and several personal failures. I realized that my earlier thought about how with all of his success he must not have experienced much failure was in error. I'd been wrong. In fact, I began to see that Dexter was a greater man because he'd gone through the sea of garbage, as he calls it. He had experienced disappointments and hurts and failures and still succeeded.

Dexter was very honest with me. He admitted that some failures were his fault. There was one couple that he said in all honesty, that he lost because he did not cultivate the wife.

He said, "Ron I did not spend time understanding what she needed out of the business but focused entirely on the husband. That taught me another lesson. If I'm going to work with a man I need to also work with his wife. I don't want to take him away from her and I don't want to create a division between them. I realized early in my business that I had to be friends with the wives as well as the husbands. I realized that we were all a team together.

"But with this one particular couple, I didn't so that. That Ron is how I learned that lesson."

The he laughed and said, "How do you learn any lesson? You learn it by messing up. You learn it by getting your face rubbed in it. You learn it by getting kicked in the gut. That's how you learn these lessons. "

Next he said, "Let's go eat! I've got somewhere new to take you today."

We jumped in his car with Birdie. I was in the backseat and Birdie and Dexter were in the front. We drove to a new cafeteria that I had never visited.

Dexter said, "You're going to like this one because the vegetables are fresh farm vegetables. Plus the food is really good."

He winked and said, "And it doesn't cost much money."

He said this because he knew that I had a weakness for eating out at expensive restaurants. He knew that I had wasted much money and lots of time going out to places that just soaked up my income. Dexter was trying, as he did with everything, to teach me something. He was teaching me that I could have a good and an enjoyable meal and still have a lot of money left over after the meal.

We sat there for nearly an hour eating and I have to admit the food was excellent. It was a cafeteria connected to an outlet mall near a park called Carrowinds Park in Charlotte, North Carolina. It was an amusement park with rides and attractions.

This cafeteria was exceptional! I went back for plate after plate until I couldn't eat anymore. Dexter ate as much as I did, and I had a wonderful time talking with him and Birdie together.

When we finished eating, Dexter said we would go back to the lake house and drop Birdie off. She was going to get a massage, while Dexter and I went out and looked at cars.

After dropping Birdie off, we made our way to a Mercedes dealership. By this time it was around 7:30 in the evening and the dealership was closed.

Dexter said, "No problem. They like people to look at their cars."

We got out and for over an hour looked around the lot at all the vehicles.

Showing great knowledge about cars, Dexter said, "This is what you need to look for."

He explained to me why these tires were better on this car and this paint job would last longer. He knew so much about cars that it amazed me. I knew that he had sold cars at one time. He had worked for a Ford dealership in New York State. Dexter had always retained his love of cars.

I asked him if I could ever afford one of these cars, what should I buy? We spent the next 30 minutes looking at different vehicles. Dexter would explain to me what would be a good car for me and what would not and why.

It is very interesting that Dexter always explained the why to me. He would say "Look at these tires. Do you know why this car has these tires?" Then he would explain why. He would say "Look at the price on this used car. Do you know why it's this price?" He would always focus on "why."

As we went through the car lot that night, I began to think back to what he had said earlier about failure. I realized that Dexter overcame many failures and many adversities and many personal disappointments, because he always had a "why." God's purpose was so real to him. God's guidance was so special that Dexter always knew why he was working and why he was doing this business. He knew why he was working with people and that means that the disappointments never did drag him down. The disappointments never permanently harmed him.

We got back in the car. By this time it was almost nine o'clock at night and as we usually did, Dexter decided to show me some lake front property. He liked going at night, because as he explained to me it was quiet and people were not around. We could take our time looking at different properties.

For the next two and a half hours, we drove from one lot to another. He took me into a new subdivision. At one point he joked with me about going to a big house at the end of the point that he thought he could get in to. But he warned me we'd better be very careful because he didn't want the police to arrest us. I didn't know at the time it was a joke.

We drove to this house and he got his flashlight. By this time it was nearly midnight and we walked up very carefully.

I was nervous and thinking, "This is a bad idea. Dexter has been wonderful and everything is in great, but I'm not sure about this one."

We got up to the deck of the house and suddenly Dexter stood up, knocked on the door and two of his Diamond leaders appeared in the window smiling.

Dexter said, "Hey! Can we come in?"

They said, "Sure Dex."

He and I went in and for the next hour and a half visited with this couple. When we left I was excited because I had been with positive, success oriented Christians who inspired me.

Dexter looked at me and said, "You know Ron, there's a reason I took you to that house."

I asked, "Why?"

Because you asked me about failure. What did you think about that house?"

I said, "It was magnificent!"

And it was. It was on the lake and beautiful.

Dexter said, "They have experienced more problems than you've ever thought about. They've overcome each of them. Don't think that your path to success is easy. Don't think that it's proof that you're in God's will if nothing bad happens. He then told me the story of all the junk this couple had overcome.

After Dexter outlined their history, he said, "But Ron, look at them now. Look at their home and their wealth and their closeness and their commitment to Christ and their togetherness. They didn't give up on each other, and they did not give up on their marriage. They did not give up on their business and look where they are now. They overcame and God blessed them and now they're there happier than they've ever been."

I realized that Dexter had furthered my education, once again. He had taken me to visit someone, but it was not just to visit. He had selected that couple as an illustration of what he was saying to me earlier about overcoming failure. He arranged our schedule so that I could have a face to face experience with a man and a woman who had successfully followed the principles he had taught me earlier. I've since learned that is typical of Dexter Yager. He is always giving you instruction, and then backing it up and using real people to teach you real lessons in life.

By this time it was two o'clock in the morning and I was beginning to tire just a bit. I tried to always be physically ready for these visits, but sometimes because of my own schedule I had a great deal to do before I arrived and wasn't always as rested as I would have liked to be. But we were still having a stimulating discussion and Dexter was still teaching me through the night.

We looked at more properties. We walked the grounds and we looked at empty houses. We shined flashlights on lake front of properties. Finally at four o'clock in the morning Dexter, as I should have expected said, "I'm hungry!"

Back to the Denny's. Back to the people who waved and said, "Dexter you're back!" Back to the all-night restaurant where we again had a big breakfast. There were pancakes and eggs and piles of bacon. We ate and ate until I thought, "Wow, I can't eat anymore."

Around five o'clock in the morning we headed back for Dexter's lake house.

Dexter leaned over to me and totally shocked me when he said, "Ron, you know I really shouldn't eat like this. I shouldn't eat this much."

He went on to say, "You know, I feel so fat."

Dexter at this time of his life was overweight. He was large in his waist. I had ignored his physical appearance because his mental and spiritual powers were so great and his personality was so exciting. But the truth was he was quite overweight. When he said, "I feel so fat." I was just startled and I thought, "What do I say? I don't want to be disrespectful to Dexter, but he brought it up.

I said, "Well Dexter if you feel fat maybe you should do something about it."

I immediately wondered if I'd gone too far.

Dexter looked over at me and said, "No Ron, you're perfectly right. Don't feel bad about saying that. I am too fat and I need to get this weight off. I need to get in better shape."

Dexter today is in fantastic physical condition. He did lose the weight. He did have some health challenges and overcame them. I'll talk about that another time. My point is that even then Dexter was deciding what to do about his physical health. Today he's a body-builder. He lifts weights and goes to the gym for regular workouts. He's dropped a large amount of weight. His waist has gone from 42 to 32 inches. He has made good his pledge of that night to do something about his weight.

Do you know what I thought that early morning, when he leaned over to me and said, "I feel so fat."? I thought, "What a remarkable man. There's no ego problem here. There's no issue with pride or arrogance. He looked over to me–a young minister—and opened his heart in saying, "I feel fat." I realized that Dexter did not have a fear of failure; whether it was health or finances or people or relationships. He just would face things and make a plan to deal with it.

He later even made a plan to overcome what at that point in his life he considered the failure of getting fat. He overcame it. He overcame it decisively, as he did everything else. During that morning I realized again what an honest and honorable person he is.

The dawn came. At 7:30 that morning, we were looking at the sparkling water and we both prayed together.

I shared with Dexter, "This has been one of my best nights with you. This has been a dawn I will never forget. This has been a special moment that has meant more to me than I can say."

Dex said, "Why Ron? What did we do that was so special this time?"

I answered him, "Dexter, you opened up your heart. You told about your failures. You told about your situations and your disappointments. You even admitted that sometimes you feel fat. Dex sometimes I feel fat. You have made me feel like I'm not alone in my struggles because you've been through them as well, and you've overcome them as well."

He said, "Ron we need to pray again. That morning we had one of the most powerful times of prayer that I had yet experienced with Dexter. He prayed for me to be protected and for my family to be sheltered. This man poured his heart out, asking God to take care of me.

Then I prayed. I asked God to help Dexter with his health and continue to use his life and continue to show him ways to be an even greater man for God.

By this time the sun had fully risen. Dawn with Dexter had come again. The night had past and in the fresh, beautiful sunlight of morning, all I could think was "Dexter is right. I don't have to be afraid of failure. I don't have to dread disappointment. I don't have to live in constant concern about what might, or might not, happen. The same God, who has brought Dexter through all of his events and navigated Dexter's life through all these situations, is the same God who loves me and wants to help me and wants to guide me as well."

We parted, Dexter to bed and me to snatch a few hours of sleep before I returned home.

On the drive back that day I thought again of all the times in my life when I messed up. I thought, "If Dexter can mess up and keep going, then I think I can keep going too. If he can lose one and find two...and if he's always moving on with a forward focus...then I can do it too. I began to realize that I was changing as a person. Things I had feared were evaporating and disappearing from my life. I had always been something of a worrier. But listening to Dexter describe how God had brought him through so many situations and to a place of wealth, success and accomplishments encouraged me that I could come through my situations as well. I began believing that I could experience God's blessings even more than I had up to that point in my life.

That was my latest dawn with Dexter. I already was eager for what was yet to come. Eager for the next day. The next dawn. The next opportunity. Before I left that morning I had already scheduled my next day with Dexter. I didn't know if any other alligators were going to come after me, but at least now I had learned principles, attitude and perspective that would help me to beat off the alligators of my life as well whenever they came.

CHAPTER 8

Success Is A Decision

I still recall the first time I knew I was being mentored. I was fifteen years old and had been asked by my father to accompany him on a special trip. He had made all the arrangements for a summer extravaganza. He had organized a two-week trip to visit the state park system in Kentucky. My mother was working at that time for the Bureau of Tourism in the state. This was her training segment and so we were free to go on our trip together.

I remember all the sights and sounds and experiences of an exceptional time with my dad. During the two weeks we took walks, rented boats, toured parks, climbed hillsides and explored caves. We finished the state park system, and then decided that we were having so much fun we would go to Mammoth Cave National Park.

We finished this wonderful trip with an opportunity to explore one of the great natural wonders of the world. This trip remains in my memory to this day. It remains not because of the scenery, or food, or recreation, but because it was the longest stretch of my life where I was being taught things by my father.

At first I did not realize his purpose. But as the trip developed I was drawn more deeply into his thinking. He taught me about finances, decision making, and planning. My dad is a very successful salesperson. When he retired from his company he was their top sales representative in the nation. So when he taught me about sales and people and relationships I learned much of great value.

When I attended Asbury College in Kentucky, I had shifted to a new mentor. The college pastor, Dr. David Seamands, took me into his orbit of influence. He was already known for his unusual ability to cut to the core of a person's life with important spiritual insight. Dr. Seamands spent many hours training me in his system of counseling. The time with Dr. Seamands proved immeasurably important for my later career. His ability to use reality counseling to help people get on track with their lives influences me to this day.

When I later attended graduate school at Asbury Theological Seminary, one of the professors had an additional impact on my life. Dr. Robert Coleman at that time was the only member of his denomination to be on Dr. Billy Graham's private steering committee for world evangelism. Dr. Coleman was known around the world as a cutting edge thinker and doer when it came to presenting the person of Jesus Christ to people who did not know him personally.

In my second year at Asbury, Dr. Coleman invited me to attend an early morning Bible study. It started every morning at 5:30 A.M. I was so hungry to know God and to know God's principals, that I eagerly agreed to the schedule. I would get up at four o'clock every morning so that I could be on time for the Bible study at 5:30. There were sometimes five or six of us, or sometimes 20 or 25. But in every morning there was an unusual presence of God and a power I had never before experienced.

One morning Dr. Coleman looked at us and said, "Gentlemen, today we are going to learn the language of heaven. Do you know what they speak in heaven?"

We all looked and waited until he continued.

"They speak the language of praise and worship to God."

Then Dr. Coleman began to lead us into a deeper understanding of the power of truly worshiping God.

Dr. Coleman became a mentor. He opened doors for me to speak up at churches and conferences. He spent many hours answering my questions and guiding my thoughts.

After seminary I became involved in the ministry of Dr. Charles Stanley in Atlanta. Some of that experience has already been examined in Chapter 1. Dr. Stanley became one of the great mentors of my life and to this day I owe him an enormous and unpayable debt of gratitude. His belief in me, his prayers for me, his training of me has been invaluable. I'm grateful to him to this day.

Now I was having a remarkable experience with Dexter Yager. I had known mentoring in the past...my father, Dr. Seamands, Dr.

Coleman, Dr. Stanley. Dexter however was different. His insights were practical and immediately usable. Not that my other mentors were not practical, because in many ways they were. What I realized though was that God, through Dexter, was giving me training and education that I'd never before encountered. God was filling in gaps in my life. I knew that if I were open and accessible he would continue to teach me through Dex.

I had learned early in my Christian experience and in my marriage relationship that stubbornness is stupid. If I determined that I did not need to know anything, then I paid the price of learning nothing. Stubbornness was not something God would bless, but openess, humility and hunger He would honor.

Recently, my son Jonathan, who is on a Little League baseball team competed for a homerun title. Out of 12 top contenders he came in fourth. He was heartbroken. The three who came in ahead of him had played for several years. Jonathan was new to the game and had only played for six weeks. I explained to him that he would do better next time.

He said, "But Dad, I tried my hardest. I tried my best. How can I try any harder?"

I said, "Jonathan trying hard is only half the battle. You also need to learn how to improve your skill; your batting; your coordination. You have to get better and not just try harder."

That's what was happening to me with Dexter. I was getting better and I was learning more. I had equal hunger for growth with my dad, Dr. Seamands, Dr. Coleman, and Dr. Stanley. I had great hunger with Dexter, but now Dexter was increasing my skill and knowledge and I wanted more. I needed to continue to be teachable. That really is a part of humility. It is the realization that you don't know everything, and I knew that there was so much more that Dexter could teach me.

My next visit with Dexter took place on a beautiful spring afternoon in the month of April. April in the Carolina's is spectacular. Flowers in bloom; birds in flight; temperature rising. It was a great time to go to the lake.

When I arrived at the house, Birdie had already left and Dexter was already up. He informed me that we needed to leave quickly because there was someone he had to speak with in another part of the city. He asked if I minded and I told him no. We left in his Mercedes convertible and we drove to the other side of Charlotte. We parked the car at a large shopping mall.

We went into the mall and went to a men's clothing shop. There waiting for us was one of Dexter's leaders. This was a new leader. He had just broken through to a higher level and Dexter had agreed to meet him to answer a question that he had. Dexter assured me that it would not take long. We went to the store to meet him and to get something cold to drink.

While we were in the store, the man said, "You know, I need a new tie."

He asked Dexter and me if we could wait a few moments while he selected some neckwear. He walked over and began to go through various options. However it took longer than anyone expected. The man looked and continued to look. He fingered one tie and then another. He tried on six, and then selected two more as possibilities.

After 25 to 30 minutes of this he finally said, "I just don't know which one to pick."

At this point, Dexter put his hand on the man's shoulder, leaned over and said, "You know a real man can make decisions. Get that tie and let's get out of here."

The man looked startled, grabbed a tie and quickly paid for it and we left. We spent the next hour at a coffee shop sipping water and soft drinks, while Dexter answered the man's questions. The man had already indicated his willingness for me to sit in and his questions had to do with very normal decisions and common situations. When we finished the man thanked both of us and left in his car while we went to Dexter's car.

When we pulled out of the parking lot Dexter said, "Ron, what do you think of what you just experienced?

I was complementary. I thanked Dexter for allowing me to be there and I expressed my appreciation for the man's willingness for me to sit in.

Dexter said, "No, that's not what I meant. What did you think of what I said to him about selecting a tie?"

I said, "Well Dexter I thought he might be embarrassed at first."

Dexter said, "I thought he might as well, but I knew I needed to kick him where he would feel it. I need to stretch him. Ron, that's a part of success. You need to stretch. Why do you think I have you bring so many questions? Why do I ask you questions in return? Why do I have you meet me and spend so many hours researching success together? Because we all need to stretch. Not just you. Not just me. Everyone."

You see," Dexter said, "people easily stay in comfort zones, where everything is easy and familiar. But in order to break through to a higher level of success something must kick them in the right place or stretch them at the right time. So in some ways, I'm a professional kicker and a professional stretcher."

But he said, "The key is that you want to learn and you're willing to learn. Success is a decision. Everything in life is a decision. I did not come into life knowing what I know now. I was not born with the right habits or the right amount of knowledge. I've had to make decisions at every point. When I said to him "a real man makes decisions" I meant that. I don't mean you make foolish decisions or I don't mean you're stupid. But what I do mean is you do need to make decisions. If success is a decision then learning to be a decision maker is critical to your success and your future.

He went on to say, "How many people Ron do you know who wallow at the level where they are? Who never move out of the pond? Who never get out of the area they are in? They remain in their comfort zone."

By this time it was 5:30 in the evening and we were going to meet Birdie in a restaurant.

Dexter said, "I've got a new place to eat. I want to introduce you to some friends and eat some where new today."

We went to a Wendy's restaurant.

Dexter said, "Wendy's, you know, is headed by a man named Dave Thomas. He has become a friend of mine. I've learned some great things about his leadership. He's an entrepreneur. He's a business leader and I'm going to go to one of his restaurants today. How about it?"

We arrived around six o'clock and Birdie was already waiting for us. We ate our sandwiches and salads and drank our cold drinks. While we sat Birdie asked me about prayer.

I had learned over the previous few visits that Birdie always seemed to have a spiritually focused question. I had begun to look forward to her questions. She would ask me about specific Bible verses. She would want to know what a particular Bible passage really meant. She would ask me about interpretations and about Biblical history. On this particular day she asked me about prayer. She asked me about effective ways to pray for other people.

Then she said, "Do you know why I'm asking you this?"

I said, "No."

She said, "Because of the list we gave you last time. Did you pray for those people?"

I have since learned that Birdie is "big" on accountability. If you agree to do something, or she asks you to do something, she wants to know if you've done it.

"Remember those 16 people on that list?" she said. "Did you pray for them?"

"Yes Birdie," I said, "I have prayed for them."

She said, "I ask because I think you ought to know what has happened to them."

She went down the list and told me what God had done and how God had worked and how God had answered prayer for many of these people.

She said, "Four of them you need to keep praying for. Here's why." She explained and we then stopped to pray. We had done this many times in cars and stores, walking by the lake, at the house and in different settings. I was getting more used to it. Dexter and Birdie would just stop and pray for people. So I prayed with them. It was a wonderful time sitting in the corner of a Wendy's restaurant praying for God to intervene in the lives of real people whom Dexter and Birdie genuinely cared about.

My purpose now is to teach you what Dexter taught me. I want you to understand the way in which we worked. Here we were having the opportunity to be together; to work together. Yet prayer was never far from what we did. Prayer was never far from what we were involved in. Dexter and Birdie would always stop to pray for people and I was always moved by the experience.

What happened next was very special. A person walked into the Wendy's just as we were finishing. This person obviously knew Dexter and Birdie and Dexter and Birdie knew them.

The person said, "Dex! Birdie! It's so great to see you!"

Dexter stood up and said to them, "What happened to a certain situation in your life?"

The person said, "It's very simple. This happened and this did not happen."

The person described what had occurred.

Dexter said, "Well let's pray for you right now."

We stopped everything and Dexter prayed specifically for this person's need and situation.

Now again, this was typical of Dexter. He would stop to pray for someone whenever that person needed prayer. Dexter would be there. Dexter would be eager to help them and communicate with them. He was eager to support them and love them and pray for them. This was not uncommon and was very special.

We left the Wendy's around 7:30 and headed back to the lake house. Dexter had bought a new piece of equipment for exercise and wanted to show it to me. When we arrived at the house, we began to pull out this item and work with it. It took about 30 minutes to position it and learn how to use it.

Dexter said, "Let's try it out!"

One thing I've learned with Dexter is that he was always ready to try something quickly. He didn't want to wait. When it was available he wanted to do it right now.

We began to do this exercise machine and for almost an hour worked out together on the machine. During the time we were working Dexter continued to teach me and continued to answer questions. There was never a down time. There was never a time when we quit or had gaps when we would stop. There was always the pursuit of knowledge and wisdom. There was always the focus of the mentor. There was always the communication of what was needed.

After we finished Dexter said, "Ron, let's talk about habits for a few minutes."

I said, "What do you mean?"

Dexter replied, "I've learned that if you have certain success habits they will save you big amounts of time and energy. For example, look at my clothes."

He said, "My shoes are always loafers. Have you noticed that"

Actually, I had noticed that every time we were together Dexter had loafers on.

He said, "Do you know why I do that? I do it because it saves me time. I don't have to tie my shoes. I don't have to worry about broken shoelaces. I can put my shoes on and they always work. They are slip on and slip off."

He went on to explain, "It may not seen to you that's an amount of time that is important. You may think that such a small amount of time is insignificant. But if you calculated how many times a day and week you put shoes on and off, you would figure out that there is more time involved in your shoes than you realize. Also it serves as a reminder to me of the value of time.

"If I consider saving a few moments by not having to lace up my shoes as valuable and important, then that continually reminds me that time itself is valuable and important. If I'm sensitive to small amounts of time, I will be more alert to large blocks of time. So I'm very careful about that, and I always make sure that I wear loafers because of the time element."

He said. "Ron let's talk about habits. It's possible, you know, to have more than one bad habit. I've noticed that at times you bite your fingernails."

I was embarrassed and nodding my head and said, "Yes. Sometimes I do Dexter. I try not to. I know it's not a good habit and doesn't look good."

Dexter said, "Ron let me tell you. I used to bite my fingernails. I used to have great amounts of nervous energy and I would bite my fingernails. One day I was with a man and learned from him that your overall appearance is a great tool in your success. That includes your fingernails. I was embarrassed as you are today. I looked at my fingernails and they didn't look good. I didn't feel happy about that.

"So I made a decision. Remember Ron, success is a decision. I made a decision and I decided that I would do something to stop biting my fingernails. I knew it was a bad habit so I decided on the following program.

"I decided that I would only bite one nail. I would choose one thumb of one hand. The only nail I would bite would be that one thumbnail. I wouldn't touch any other nail and if I felt the need to bite a fingernail I would only bite that one nail.

"What that did for me was it made me stop biting the other nails and focused me on the one thumb nail. Then over time, when I achieved control over my habit, I only had one thumbnail to stop biting. Just the one was not as hard for me to stop biting as the effort it would have been to stop biting all the nails at once.

"I made a decision and created a plan and I followed the plan after my decision. Everything started Ron with the decision. Do you understand that?"

I nodded yes and I thought to myself, "This is remarkable. I never would have thought of a plan like this."

While Dexter explained his approach to breaking the habit a biting fingernails, I had been writing down his plan in detail. I wanted to try it as well.

Dexter said, "Whether it's shoes or fingernails, everything starts with a decision and becomes a habit. That's why it is important for you have the right habits and for you to develop the right patterns."

He said, "I wear shorts with large pockets because the pockets give me room to carry things with me. I have certain types of shorts that work for me and I only buy those shorts. I don't waste my time looking for different styles, or different types. I know what works for me and I work with what works. I find out what works and I don't get away from it. I stick to it.

"Ron do you see what I mean about habits? They start with decisions. Then when you decide on the right habit, the right habit will carry you to greater success."

I continued to write as Dexter said, "I've talked about shorts, and loafers and fingernails. What about scheduling? Do you see that I follow a pattern in my schedules. I get up at a certain time and I go to bed at a certain time and I eat at certain time. I don't have to debate that. I know what works for me. I've thought it through very carefully, and I know what works and I followed that. After all Ron, you don't want to reinvent the wheel. If it works, it works."

Next Dexter said, "Does that mean that I'm not open to new things? No, it just means that I know what patterns help my performance and I know what things drag me down. So I try always to follow patterns that I have proven and that I have tested and I know work. I don't just jump in and do anything. I think first. Before I decide, I think."

He said, "Let's call it think; decide; habit."

I quickly wrote that down.

135

I thought, "WOW! Here is a formula that I can use in my own life. Think it through. Make a decision. Create a habit. Then I added a fourth, follow that habit.

Dexter then began to describe to me how hard it had been for him in the past to learn certain things.

He said, "Ron I was shy. I was not comfortable talking to people on the phone. So I made myself learn to talk on the phone. I developed a good telephone habit because I knew I needed that. You see, not everything that comes naturally is going to work for you. You may need to change what comes naturally to you if you want to succeed in life."

He said, "I remember a woman who wrote me a check early in the business and the check bounced. I thought well okay, that could happen to anybody. I gave her another chance, and she wrote another check that bounced. I remember when I asked her about it she said, 'I've never been good at accounting. I guess I'm still not very good at it.'"

Dex said, "I was very nice to her and I helped her with her finances and I helped her with their business. But I always thought about what she said and it made me realize that if you're not good at something, and you have a business, you had better learn to be good at it. I have tried over the years to determine what I needed to be good at and then to learn those things. Once I've learned them I turn them into patterns and then into habits and then I stick to those habits. When I do this I can use my energy for other things."

He said, "There are certain things I do every day. I don't question them. They work for me. If they work for me, I then can use my energy to work on other things in other situations where I don't have patterns or habits."

By this time it was 11 o'clock at night and Dexter had been talking for hours. He never really slowed down at any point during our times together. He always had something new to say and some insight to give and some knowledge to share. Sometimes it was amazing how he could go such lengths without repeating himself and without missing the target with me. He always seemed to know what I needed and how I needed it delivered.

At 11:30 Dexter said, "Let's go out. Let's drive around for a while. We followed his pattern: into the car; driving around the lake;

looking at property. At 3:30 in the morning we went to the all-night Denny's and sat as everyone greeted Dexter and came over to ask how he was doing. We had our pancakes and eggs and other items.

Then at 4:30 a.m. Dexter stood and stretched and said, " Hey Ron, why don't we go for a walk?"

I needed the walk at this point. It had been another tremendous night. I had learned so much more than I expected. I already had written down a number of areas where I needed new habits and success patterns. I knew that what Dexter had taught me would have a great impact and benefit in my life, if I put it into practice. I was a little stiff and tired and when he suggested a walk I thought it was a great idea.

We walked outside of his house after we returned from the restaurant. We walked around his property in the late-night, early morning hours, for several minutes. I was just beginning to wake up and the blood was flowing again.

Dexter said, "Hey, I don't think we really figured out that exercise machine. Let's go back and try it again."

So at five o'clock in the morning we went back to the room and tried out the new device again. Dexter was like a kid at Christmas. He thought this device was really cool. He wanted to learn everything about it. So for another 45 minutes, we worked with the machine, while Dexter continued to answer my questions and discuss insights and answers.

At 6:30 in the morning the sun was just beginning to glimmer over the horizon. The sky was beginning to lighten and the water was beginning to sparkle. By seven o'clock we were out on the deck and stood watching geese skim the water.

Dexter turned to me and said, "Ron, now if you have any more questions this is a good time for it. There's nothing like this time of day to relax and open your heart and your mind. If you have anything else then I'm ready. Let's have it."

As a matter-of-fact I did have something else. I said, "Dexter you said that you were not born this way. You had to develop habits and learn to make decisions. Please explain that to me. What did you do that made you different?"

He said, "Ron when I was 12 years old I decided that I needed to make more money. I bought soft drinks; put them in ice and took them to some guys who were working construction. I sold so many soft drinks that I decided this would be a great business opportunity. I went back for more the next day. For sometime after that, I developed an ongoing business with these construction guys. They would look forward to my coming and I would sell them drinks every morning. I was just a kid, but I made so much extra money that I was able to buy a car. The only problem was I was too young to drive it. My dad would not allow me to drive the car, no matter what I said."

He said, "Ron, I don't know how early this started for me, but at some point I knew I wanted success. I knew I wanted security. I knew I wanted independence and freedom and I knew I had to work to get it. Even back then, as a kid, I wanted to learn how to achieve things. Maybe it came from my parents, maybe it came from somebody I don't even remember. There was a seed planted in me early and it's been sprouting all my life. I have been raking in the harvest all these years. But it started back then,"

He said, "There were many things I needed to change. There was so much I knew I needed to know. There were several points in my life when I made a decision..."

I realized again at that point how critical decision-making is to the whole process of success.

He said, "I made a decision at several points in my life that I needed to learn this, or that I needed to change that. I would realize I needed to experience this, or I needed to understand that. But every change in every experience started with a decision.

So Ron success really is a decision. You can have hunger and vision and desire, but without the decision, it's like living in a dreamland."

He said, "Do you know the difference between a dream and a fantasy?"

By this time the sun was up and the dawn was breathtaking. Light and color were everywhere. I stood on the deck looking at Dexter and I said, "Tell me, please. What is the difference between a dream and fantasy?"

He replied, "It's very simple. A dream is something you are willing to work for. A dream is something you're willing to fight for. A dream is something you're willing to plan for and try for. It's a dream, and it's within reach, and you can do it.

"Fantasy however is a dream that you're not willing to work for. All you do is fantasize and imagine what life would be like if you had this, or did that. But with a fantasy you never get off your bottom and do anything about it. You never get up and go. You never work for it. You never fight for it. So all your life, it's just a fantasy.

"I knew early in my life, that if I was going to have dreams, I could not allow them to become fantasies. The difference between a dream and a fantasy is a decision. Do you understand that? The difference between a dream and a fantasy is a decision. That's why I say that success is a decision. Isn't everything a decision?"

He said, "When you asked Jesus into your heart as your Savior, wasn't that a decision?"

I nodded yes.

He went on to say, "When you decided that you were in love with Amy and wanted to marry her, was that a decision?"

I again nodded yes.

"When you had your daughter Allison, was that a decision?"

I nodded yes again. (We had not had Jonathan at that point. Allison was our only child.)

Dex said, "Ron everything is a decision. Even failure is a decision. People think they fail because they're not good enough or they didn't work hard enough. The truth is they didn't dream big enough. They didn't decide to do something.

"Whenever you make a decision, that's where a dream starts to become a reality. That's where a dream is no longer a fantasy. It's then something different and something special. That's the point where it can become real in your life. That's why I say that success is a decision and everything depends on your making the right decision.

"I've talked tonight about habits and patterns, but every habit and every pattern that I've described started with a decision. It's like the guy in the mall, he took all that time searching for a tie. He spent a half-hour of time that I was giving him in a special arrangement with you. It was really your time. He actually stole the time. He was a thief of your time and my time because he couldn't make a decision.

"Do you see how important it is that you know how to make a decision? That you know how to stand up like a man and do something about your dreams?"

Then Dex looked at me and said, "Well, how about it? Does that cover everything for today?"

It was eight o'clock in the morning, and I knew that he was nearing his bedtime. It was almost time for him to retire. I was ready to call it a night, or a day. I'm still not sure which.

We walked into the kitchen, had some high fiber oatmeal raisin cookies and drank some water and then had our prayer together. It wouldn't have been right to leave without the prayer.

Dexter prayed for everybody else, and he always prayed for me, and I always prayed for him. We finished the prayer.

He went to bed and I went to sleep. Later that day I slipped out quietly and carefully while Dexter and Birdie slept. I was already looking forward to my next dawn with Dexter.

CHAPTER 9

Have Fun While You Succeed

I didn't always go to Dexter for serious reasons. Sometimes I went just to enjoy his company. There was one occasion when I arrived with very few questions and not much of an agenda. Dexter had told me on the previous visit that he wanted to show me something that I would enjoy and to plan for extra time to have some fun. I honestly did not know what Dexter meant by fun, but I was about to find out.

When I arrived at the lake house, there were other leaders already present. I knew Dexter on occasion had meetings that overlapped with mine and so I was not surprised.

Dexter walked into the kitchen where I was waiting and said, "Ron go change clothes, we're going on the boat today."

Dex had more than one boat but I noticed that when he said "the boat" there was something about the way he said it.

I walked into the bedroom and there were swimming trunks and a T-shirt, which I quickly changed in to. I came out and walked down to the dock that was attached to his property. It was a hot summer day. It was perfect for water sports. The boat that he referred to turned out to be a new speed boat with, as he told me, Corvette engines.

"This boat," he said, "is so fast you won't believe it until you ride on it."

Several of us got into the boat. Dexter was at the front and prepared to take us on a speed trip down Lake Wylie. He wore a T-shirt with shorts and his usual casual loafers. Today he also had on a pair of black Ray Ban sunglasses.

We were quickly out in the middle of the lake. There was a long straight stretch of water and Dexter said, "Watch this!"

He pushed the throttle forward and all of us tumbled into the back of the boat. No one expected the power that would be exhibited. The boat quickly was running at the equivalent of around 80 to 90 mph. We could not even talk with the wind so violently in our faces. I still remember the fun of that sun drenched afternoon.

We spent three hours on the lake. Dexter had prepared everything. Sunscreen was available and towels were positioned. Places to stop had been arranged. The whole afternoon was a rollicking good time.

We stopped at one dock to fuel. Everyone knew Dexter. I was no longer surprised at this. Dexter went out and spoke with the owner of the marina for a few minutes while the boat was refueled. We all went into the store to purchase snacks and water. When we came back to the boat, Dexter was ready to go and we rapidly made our way down the lake.

At the end of the 3½ hour recreational ride, we were back at the lake house tired, relaxed, sun burnt and happy. Dexter had arranged for some food to be brought in. It was already waiting for us.

Mostly my times with Dexter were times of teaching and seriousness. They were times of mentoring and development. But this was an example of Dexter at his fun loving best. Dexter always made everything a good time. Even in our serious moments together, there was always an element of fun and enjoyment. Today I could tell was going to be special. And it certainly was.

We spent time relaxing after the boat ride; eating burgers and preparing for the evening. Two of the leaders were going to stay until eight o'clock and I had already been alerted to the change in schedule.

Dexter said, "Why don't we watch some TV?"

We went into the living room and watched some hilarious videos that he had rented. They were of comedians that he was planning to have for some of his large convention opportunities. He wanted to review them and invited us to review them with him.

It was great fun laughing. One man was so hilarious as he dropped water melons from a tall building, that we rolled on the floor in delight at his antics. After reviewing four comedians, Dexter then lead us in the discussion of what we liked and what we did not like.

He wanted to know who we thought would be great for a crowd at one of his large free enterprise celebrations.

By the time 8 o'clock arrived, the other two leaders were preparing to leave. I was getting ready for my night owl session with Dexter, until the coming of the dawn. We stood for a moment in the doorway. All of us were relaxed and happy and Dexter did as he always did. He prayed with and for the other two leaders who were present. It was obvious that they were deeply touched.

After Dexter prayed for them he leaned down and to everyone's surprise pinched one of the men on the shoulder. The man jumped and then laughed a hearty laugh and said, " Dexter, it's so great to have fun! I feel like a kid again."

Dexter said, "I wouldn't have done that if I hadn't known it was okay with you."

We all laughed again and the two men were on their way.

After they left Dexter turned to me and said, "Did I surprise you with the pinch?"

I said, "Well yes, a little bit."

He said, "I've been working with this particular man for a long time. He's always been serious and always had trouble relaxing. I received a call from his wife recently, and she said, 'Dexter I'm worried about my husband. He's too tense. He never unwinds. He's always driving for the next goal and he never relaxes.'

"I decided I would try to relax him. That's why I arranged today. That's why we went on the boat. That's why we watched the comedians. I had a plan the whole time, even the pinch was part of my plan. You noticed I didn't pinch anybody else. I just pinched him. After talking to his wife I knew that he needed to not take himself so seriously."

I thought for a moment of the earlier discussion we had had on one of my previous visits. It was the time when Dexter had talked about how to know your players. Dexter once again had shown shrewd insight into the personality of a particular person.

It was 8:30 by now and Dexter said, "Let's go eat again."

Birdie met us upstairs and we left and arrived at a late-night Italian restaurant. I'd not been to an Italian restaurant yet with Dexter and was excited about the change of pace. He'd just met the owner of this particular place and had been impressed with their food and positive attitude. He had already met the cooks and the waiters and waitresses and most of the customers who were regulars. Now he was bringing me for an Italian feast.

It was a great night. After the boat and the comedians I was very hungry. We sat around a large table and people came and went. Individuals would stop and speak to Dexter and he would chat with them for a moment and ask how they were doing. Everyone seemed to know him even though this was a relatively new place that Dexter had discovered.

The food was outstanding. I ate more than I needed and loved every bite. Dexter and I talked about spiritual questions that Birdie had brought up earlier. Her questions again were about the Bible's teachings on particular topics. We spent an hour and a half discussing questions and answers about scriptural situations, all the while eating and laughing. It was one of the most enjoyable times I'd ever had with Dexter, or anyone else for that matter.

We went back to the house at 10:30. There was a car in the driveway that I did not recognize. I wondered for a moment if Dexter had scheduled someone else I did not know about.

Dexter only smiled and unlocked the door for us to go in. There was an individual waiting for us in a special room.

Dexter said, "I've made a special arrangement for you Ron. I think you'll like this."

It was a massage therapist. She'd arrived earlier than us and prepared a table. When I looked around at first, I'd thought it must be for Birdie or Dexter.

Dexter said, "No Ron. Tonight this is for you. Have you ever had a professional massage?"

I said, "Dexter I've never had one. I'd sure like to try it though."

He said, "Well tonight is your night. I've arranged for a special time with this lady who is an excellent therapist. I've already paid her. I even paid her extra to come out at night, because I knew we wouldn't be here until late. She's going to give you a two hour massage. I want you to start right and always know what a great massage is really like."

I was nervous. I'd never been in a situation like this before. I was a physically shy pastor who almost didn't go to the beach.

With some trepidation, I undressed in another room and placed a towel around me and came back out into the workout room. I laid on the table and as Dexter talked to me the therapist began the two hour massage therapy.

Dexter talked as I drifted in and out of consciousness. I'd never been so physically relaxed in my life. I was amazed at the physical and emotional benefits I was already experiencing. This was beyond anything I'd ever imagined.

At the end of the two hours I was ready to go to sleep. Dexter, however, was not.

He said, "Okay Ron go on into the bathroom and get dressed and then we'll go out and look at some more properties."

I shook off my drowsiness, walked into the bathroom; showered and dressed. When I came back out of the room the table and the therapist were gone.

I thanked Dexter and said, "Dexter I don't know what this must have cost, but this was great. Can I pay anything?"

He said, " Don't worry about it. This was my gift to you. You've used large amounts of your time and you've spent your money coming to see me and I appreciate that. I wanted to give something extra back to you tonight."

Remember, I'd never had a professional massage before in my life. I knew at that moment that I wanted to have many more. It was one of the most outstanding physical relaxations I'd ever experienced. I could not wait for the next time.

We got into his car and drove to look at more property. Dexter had already told me that there was a special piece of property he wanted me to see. We arrived there at 1:30 in the morning. I'd never felt better in my life. The time in the boat; the food by the dock; the hilarious presentations of the comedians; the Italian dinner; the two hour massage. It was wonderful!

Now Dexter was showing me property that I could actually live on. He was showing me a small house that I might be able to buy. I still wasn't certain I wanted to move to North Carolina as I had a great love for my hometown in Kentucky. But it just seemed as if everything was focused on my own enjoyment on that special night. Dexter is great fun to be with. He is endlessly interesting and always positive. But tonight, he had added a special dimension to my life.

Since those early days of Dexter I have made many trips with he and Birdie. My first trip to Europe was with Dexter and Birdie and my wife Amy. We flew into the Brussels Airport. I'd never been on an international flight. I'd never even been an on all-night flight.

We arrived in the morning and leaders were there to pick us up. Dexter and Birdie wanted breakfast. We went to a small cafe in a tiny Dutch town and had Birdie's favorite European meal—Mussels.

I ate eggs and "french fries," although I realized they were actually Belgian and Dutch fries for that morning. Amy had a small meal and Dexter and Birdie seemed to be at the top of the world. They were so happy.

I went to the restroom and when I came out, everyone was gone. Here I was, having left the Belgian Airport and crossed into Holland to a strange village. I spoke only English. I had no luggage, as it all was in the car. I was all alone. Even my wife was gone. What was I going to do?

I walked outside and no one was there. I looked up and down the street and it was abandoned. I knew we were going in a particular direction when we'd stopped, so I started to walk that way.

After a few minutes, a car quickly pulled out of a side street. A window rolled down and Dexter roared with laughter and said, "Hey Ron! Do you need a ride?"

Everybody was smiling. I jumped into the car and I realized they had enjoyed playing a joke on me. It was always like that. Dexter would play tricks. He would tell jokes. He would laugh and do something, unexpectedly enjoyable.

We would have great times together for the next two years. I spent a great deal of time with Dexter in Europe. He and I and Amy and Birdie went to Korea together. We went throughout England, doing meetings together. Everywhere we went we had wonderful fun.

Amy, Allison, and I were in a restaurant in London, on one occasion, with Dexter and Birdie. It was late at night. The restaurant was about to close.

We'd just finished our dessert, wonderful French pastries, when Dexter said, "Let's take a walk."

The walk extended until three o'clock in the morning. We went up and down the fascinating London streets looking at architecture and enjoying the post midnight scenery. At 3 o'clock in the morning we went back to our hotel in Mayfair and stood in the lobby for moment as Dexter and Birdie both expressed their appreciation for our spending time with them in the British capital.

Allison was dazzled. She felt so welcomed by Dexter and Birdie. She knew that it was special and she had been freely included. Dexter is like that. He includes everyone. If someone wanted to go with us Dexter would often say "Come on" and also invite the children and spouses of the leaders we were with. Dexter always entertained us with fascinating stories and hilarious accounts of adventures he'd had with different individuals.

I still remember one night in Germany when Dexter, thirty of his friends, Amy and I and Birdie were in a restaurant. Dexter pulled out a paper coaster from underneath his soft drink. It was thick and circular and Dexter flipped it like a flying saucer across the room. It struck one of the leaders. The leader looked around startled not knowing what had happened. Quietly, as everything settled back into its normal rhythm Dexter slung another coaster at another person who looked startled and confused.

For 15 minutes Dexter cautiously and discreetly sent these tiny cardboard flying saucers flying throughout the room until everyone was looking and wondering what in the world was going on.

Well, what in the world was going on was very simple. Dexter was having fun with all of us. No one suspected him. He was the senior leader of the group. No one ever thought he would be responsible for these events.

Then someone saw him throw the coaster. I still think that he did it on purpose and wanted to be caught. When everyone saw him, there is a moment of total silence.

Then, as if by a signal, the entire room erupted into gales of laughter. Men and women laughed until they fell from their chairs. For 15 full minutes people laughed and a roared their approval of Dexter's trick. Dexter grinned and knew that he had given this crowd a memorable, fun experience.

That's what I say when I remind you that Dexter is not always serious. He is fun. Whether it was on a special day when he had arranged for fun activities, such as the boat, or the food, or the massage, he is fun.

Or whether it is just in the normal ins and outs of everyday life, Dexter has a healthy sense of humor. It shows frequently. I will admit, there are also times when he is mischievous and will gain great pleasure from playing a practical joke on you.

One night in a motor home in Germany, we were traveling between rallies. There were several of us sleeping in the RV as we traveled. I went into the rear bathroom for a moment and took out my wallet and placed it on a shelf. When I walked out of the bathroom I forgot that I had left the wallet on the shelf. Dexter went in after me and came out a few minutes later.

About 20 minutes further into the ride I missed my wallet. When I returned to the bathroom, the wallet was gone. I panicked. I was in a strange country. Everything I had was in that wallet.

I frantically looked through every cabinet and on every shelf in the bathroom. I came out and asked if anyone had seen my wallet. People responded with a blank stare and a negative shaking of the head.

After almost half an hour of intense concern Dexter walked up and handed me my wallet. He said, "Now Ron, I started this as a joke. I thought you would walk right back in and need your wallet. Then I would seem innocent for a moment, but I would give it to you. It would just be a joke."

He said, "I'm not cruel and I didn't keep it to be mean to you and I didn't let you look for it this long just to make a joke. I had another thought after I saw the wallet. I realized that you had carelessly done something that could create a real problem for you as you travel. I decided to keep the wallet for a little extra time so that you would always remember the loss of it and it would help you not to do it again."

He said, "If you were by yourself somewhere, or in a restaurant with us, and without thinking laid your wallet down that could be a small disaster for you. I would not want that to happen."

"Although," at this point he winked at me, "it was a very tempting joke at the beginning." And he laughed.

I laughed as well. More out of relief, than anything else, for the return of my wallet. I even was mildly irritated for a moment but then I paused and I realized that he was doing what he always did. He was teaching me; training me; mentoring me; protecting me. I felt a rush of gratitude for his commitment to always improve me as a person.

My trips with Dexter have always been enjoyable. The trips with he and Birdie have always been fun. I've never had an excursion with them that I did not enjoy. My wife Amy has a scintillating, fun personality. Amy does not naturally get depressed. She is positive and exuberant and excited most of the time. She is fabulous to live with and she has told me for years that some of the most enjoyable moments of her life have been our times together with Dexter and Birdie Yager. She recognizes the same fun focus in them that lives in her.

It's true. Dexter is not always serious and intense and goal centered. Sometimes, he just relaxes and has fun. And when he does have fun, he makes sure that it is fun for everyone else. Dexter never allows a joke to get out of control. He doesn't do anything that is cruel, or harmful. He only pulls jokes on people whom he already knows can handle them. Because of that, things don't ever get out of hand, or out of control.

The night that I'd had the massage, and the boat ride, and the comedians was an especially enjoyable night. But every time we were together something fun occurred, or something hilarious happened, or Dexter told me some story that made me laugh for several minutes after the telling. It was not unusual to have times like this.

The night of the massage was exceptional, because he had arranged so many fun things to do. He must have thought when he planned our time together that I needed a different kind of night; that I needed a change of pace; that I needed a bit more fun than usual.

After we looked at the property that I previously mentioned, we arrived at the lake house at 6:30 a.m. I was very relaxed. The massage therapy was still having its positive effect on me.

Dexter said, "Why don't we sit and talk for a few more minutes, while the sun comes up."

I had already begun to look forward to this time of the morning because during my dawns with Dexter, the dawn itself had always been a special moment of bonding and understanding with him. So when he said, "Let's sit and watch the sun come up" I was happy to do so.

We sat for a few minutes and watched the sun beginning to lighten the sky. Dexter said, "Ron, you know, people have to know how to reward themselves. For me, having fun is a reward. For me having fun is a benefit. I realize that other people need that as well."

He said, "If everything is grim and determined you'll crack up after a while. I heard a man tell a story once about an archery bow. He was a preacher and he was warning us not to be too "strung out," or too intense to remember to relax.

"I remember the sermon. The preacher said that even Jesus, the Son of God, would go away and relax or take time away for himself and rest. He then gave the example of a bow. If you keep a bow strung too long, it hurts the bow. It's true that the bow should strung tightly and correctly if you're going to be able to use that bow to send an arrow successfully into the bull's-eye or the target."

"But," Dex said, "the preacher reminded all of us that if you don't unstring the bow and you keep it too tight for too long, it will lose its power and will be bad for the bow. It also will be useless for hitting the target.

"Ron, I always want you to be able to hit your target. That means that you need to be able to sometimes unstring your bow," he said.

We had a great time growing and praying and learning together. Sometimes it's been very serious. But we always need to have fun."

He said, "Do you have fun with Amy?"

I said, "Yes I do. She's great fun to be with."

Dexter said, "Never forget that. She needs it and you need it. What about your children? They need it as well. They want a dad who can laugh and relax. A dad they know wants to have fun with them."

He said, "You know, it's the same with the people in your business group. If you're going to build a big business, then people must want to be with you. People must need their time with you. You need to teach them and stretch them and help them to grow. But you always want to make sure that they enjoy your time together.

"I've been watching you during our last few visits. I thought on this particular night, you needed a little extra. That's why I did it. I wanted to make sure that you continue to grow, by continuing to relax."

I said, "Dexter, I've never heard you put it like that before. Continue to grow by continuing to relax."

Dexter said, "Ron remember everything in life is a balance. You don't want to go to extremes on anything. You don't want to relax all the time. You don't want to have fun all the time. And, you don't want to be serious all the time. You need a balance between the two and that is what I've tried to do on this visit together."

By this time it was 7:30 in the morning. The sun was blazing over the horizon and it was another fantastic dawn on Lake Wiley. I'd had one of the most fun days I'd had with anyone in years.

We both stood.

Dexter said, "Ron, we need to pray and get you ready to sleep so you'll be safe to drive back."

He said, "When you come back, we're going to do something special. We're going to play some games. I want to show you some new ways to learn. We'll play checkers together and we'll do some fun games. Even when you have questions and even when you're serious, we'll still have a good time together."

Then we prayed, as we always did, and he asked God to protect me and to give his angels charge over me as I traveled later that day. He prayed for Amy and my family. I prayed for he and Birdie and his children and grandchildren and people around the world to be influenced for God.

He then smiled and went to his room. I returned to the guest room, and lay down utterly relaxed, and entirely content.

When I woke several hours later, I had my usual oatmeal raisin cookie and bottled water. I drove home eager to have fun with my family after my happy dawn with Dexter.

CHAPTER 10
Plan Now To Win Later

W hen I returned to Dexter's for my next visit, I had already been wondering what he meant by "Be prepared to play checkers." On all of our previous visits, we had never played any games at all.

When I arrived the afternoon of my new visit Dexter was still asleep. I decided to take a walk. I walked around the grounds beside the lake and enjoyed the beauty of the location and the warmth of the weather. After nearly an hour of waiting I returned to the house. Birdie was working on answering mail and was on the phone with an assistant. Dexter was still asleep.

After a few more minutes Birdie leaned over and said to me, "He only got to bed around 10 o'clock this morning, so if you don't mind waiting a bit longer, that would be great."

I nodded yes and settled in for a wait. I had brought books with me, so I sat on a chair looking out at the water and read for another half an hour.

By the time Dexter walked in it was almost four o'clock in the afternoon. Dexter apologized for the delay and said that he'd had an unusually late phone conference that had taken much more time than he had expected. Then Dexter, as he always did, sat and began to teach me a lesson. This is what I'd learned to expect from my time with him, and today was no exception.

As we sat and talked Dexter explained that it is important to not only work hard, but to think correctly. He explained that the phone conference he had been involved in had been particularly demanding. He was in the process of trying to help two men with a difficult situation. He explained the circumstances to me without revealing the identity of the two men.

Then he said, "Ron, isn't it amazing how a person can be intelligent, educated and experienced, and still do some of the dumbest things?"

He laughed and said, "Now I am no exception. I have done some dumb things myself. I have made big mistakes, but I always determined to learn from those mistakes. The two men I was speaking with last night both had made foolish decisions. They knew better. When they discussed the situation with me last night, they admitted that they knew better and they were moaning and groaning over the fact that they had messed up and they could not understand why they had been so dumb.

"I told them it's human nature to allow your emotions to rule over your logic. I decided early in my life, and early in the development of my business, to at least try to put logic first. I have not always succeeded, but I've tried to be a thinker.

"Years ago, when Birdie had a job working with information and technology, I would drive around late at night and pray and think. Birdie worked long hours and I had time on my hands. During this period of our lives, I spent great amounts of time trying to learn the art of analysis. I tried to learn how to break down situations into logical parts. I tried to learn to look at situations without too much emotion. What these two guys did in their circumstance was to make decisions based on what they wanted to happen, not on reality. That's not logical."

Then Dexter leaned forward and made a statement that I have to this day never forgotten, and never gotten over.

He completely surprised me by saying, "You know Ron, people are basically stupid."

When he said this, he must have noticed the startled reaction on my face. Dexter had always been polite and thoughtful in all of his comments about other people. He'd never been rude or unkind comments and here he was calling people basically stupid. He knew that I was puzzled and he waited while I decided how to ask my question. I could just see the beginning of a small smile at the edge of his mouth and suddenly I was aware that Dexter had set me up. He had deliberately made a provocative statement so that I would be blown

RON BALL

out of my mental comfort zone and would get a point that I might not have grasped any other way. So I took the bait.

I said, "Dexter, what do you mean that people are stupid?"

Dexter knew he had me so he plunged in.

He said, "Ron, people are not always logical. They are not always rational. As I said a moment ago, many people make decisions based on their emotional needs of the moment. Take a purchase for example. I talked to a man once who wanted to build a business under me. He was sharp, hard-working and had a good personality. But he had problems handling his money. In this particular case, he wanted to buy a boat.

"He came to me, and he said, "Here's the boat I want. I think this would be a great reward for me and my family."

I told him, "You don't have the money to buy the boat. You can't afford it. You should build your business so big that buying the boat will not only be a reward, it will be no financial problem at all.

"Now what do you think he did? He bought the boat. It was an expensive boat and he went into debt to buy it. Then I noticed that he was no longer coming to business meetings. So I called him and he told me that he wanted to build a business and that he wanted to be free, but he just did not have the extra money to travel and work on his business group.

"Where did that extra money go? It went into the water with his boat. That's dumb. That's what I mean, when I say that people are basically stupid.

"I don't mean that people are dumb as a put down. I'm not saying that to be critical of people. I am not trying to be negative toward people. I'm trying to help you see something about how to think."

Then Dexter said, "I believe that if God has called me to anything, he has called me to be an educator to help people's thinking. Ron look at your background in the church. You've been a pastor, you've been to seminary, you've preached for a few years."

He said, "What did you think awhile back when I told you that most churches tend to be socialist in their thinking?"

Well this was my turn, and I said, "Dexter I gave that serious thought and I have to agree that is a problem with many churches."

Dexter leaned forward and said, "I'm not saying that is a problem in all churches. But I do think that there are many churches where people are brought up to believe that God should just automatically do something for them without any effort or commitment or belief or obedience on their part. They believe God is going to drop success in their laps, and when it doesn't happen they fill their life with excuses. They say life is not fair, or God has not been fair to me. They come up with any number of reasons why things are just not fair. But they continue in their laziness, or their lack of effort, and they produce their own results."

At this point Dexter leaned back and I knew we were in for a long conversation. I did not mind. I wanted the long conversation, because Dexter was probing deeply into the wisdom of life and success. I knew that this is what I'd come for. I did not want anything to derail his momentum. I listened intently as he talked.

He continued, "Ron, I am concerned that Christians especially learn to outwork, out think, and out love everybody else. We have the Savior; we have the Bible; we have God's holy truth, and we should be an example of the best of the best. I know that I fail. I know that I don't always measure up to what God wants me to be, but I have a commitment to excellence, and that commitment honors the Lord."

He said, "When I say I'm an educator, what I mean is this. People don't think clearly and people don't think logically. People make, as I said earlier, emotional decisions based on what they want and what they need. They don't always make them on what is right or logical. My job is to try to push their thinking in the right direction based on God's principals in the Bible. I know I'm a businessman and I work with business. But I'm also Christian and I want God's principals to fill my business and my work. I know when I stand before people in a business meeting what they really need to know is 'How do I think correctly about life; about success; about God; about anything that matters to them?' I'm an educator and I may not always get it right. I may not always succeed, but my purpose and my aim is to help people think correctly."

By this time Dexter had been talking and explaining for nearly two hours. It was six o'clock in the evening and Dexter suggested that we continue the conversation over dinner. Birdie had finished her work and had changed clothes and was ready to go out. We returned to the Italian restaurant we had visited on our previous time together.

156

As usual, everyone knew Dexter and seemed genuinely happy to see he and Birdie. Birdie spent a few minutes talking with the owner of the restaurant about some people they were bringing in later in the week to eat. Dexter and I sat and talked more about his ideas concerning how people think.

When we had finished an outstanding meal of freshly made pasta and tomato sauce with mounds of garlic bread, Dexter leaned back and said, "Let's talk more about how to think."

Dexter said, "Thinking is the root of behavior. If you don't think right, you'll not do right. For example, if you think that being married but sleeping with other women is all right then that will influence your temptation to go do it. If you really think that's okay, even though it's not, then you are more likely to do it. If you give into that temptation you'll mess up your family, and you'll ruin your life. But it all started in your thinking.

"So I look at everyone and I ask the questions 'What do they need to think to live life the right way? What do they need to think to be successful?' So I teach them about hard work. I teach them to have a great positive attitude."

Dex explained, "I believe that people need a positive attitude, not some of the time, or most of the time, but all of the time. I believe people need a positive attitude, especially when they don't think they need it. So I teach them how to think positive thoughts. I teach them how to think always in terms of belief and success. Even the Bible says, 'As you think in your heart, so are you.' So I teach them to have positive thoughts. I teach them about delayed gratification."

I had heard Dexter use this term on other occasions so I was ready for it this time.

Dexter continued, "Delayed gratification means that you look down the road and you see your ultimate destination. You make the decisions and do the actions now that will get you where you want to be later. If that means delaying your gratification and delaying your rewards and delaying your situation so that you can get something bigger and better later on...then that's smart. To not do that is stupid. So I teach people delayed gratification."

I realized that Dexter was giving me a seminar on success.

We sat in the restaurant for two more hours. It was nearly nine o'clock before Dexter and Birdie finally decided that it was time to go. It was a nice evening, and Dexter put the convertible top down on the Mercedes.

We got into the car and as the top went down Dexter said, "Let's take Birdie back to the house and then talk some more."

We drove back on a very pleasant evening and arrived at the lake house at 9:30. I knew that Dexter wanted to teach me certain things that day. He had not even asked me what my questions were. He had begun teaching me the moment that he walked in the room after waking from sleep, and had continued until the moment when we arrived at the lake house. Birdie went downstairs to her bedroom and Dexter and I continued the conversation.

Dexter said, "Ron I want to show you something that will help you understand what I'm saying."

I said, "Great! Go right ahead."

Dexter then surprised me by pulling out a checkerboard and a box of checker pieces. I had not played checkers since I was a child. I enjoyed the game, but had not played it for many years. Dexter laid the board on a table and placed all the checkers in their proper positions.

He said, "Ron, now you may think that this is a distraction from what we've been doing, but it's not. I'm going to use this game to show you something. Let's play for a few minutes and then I'm going to ask you some questions."

We began to play checkers. We played 11 games in a row before I won a game. On game 12, I finally and barely won.

Dexter looked up and said, "Ron why do you think I won 11 straight games before you won a game?"

I said, "Well, could it be that you play checkers a lot? Could it be that you play and have experience and I don't?"

He laughed and said, "No, that's not it at all. I only started playing checkers again about two weeks ago and I don't play a lot. I've not played for years, but I still was able to beat you almost every game. There's a reason. What do you think that reason is?"

I could not come up with an answer. I was embarrassed for a moment because I knew he wanted me to come up with my own understanding. But I just could not get it.

Dexter finally said, "All right. This is what happened."

He said, "I am a long term thinker. You already know that. I'm always thinking into the future and planning what can happen as a result of what I do now. Because I have so disciplined my mind to think long term and to look at cause and effect and to look at results, that's the way I play checkers as well. You play checkers the way most people play checkers. You just make a move and then that move dictates the next move and that move determines the next move and that move brings you to the next move. But you don't have a plan. You don't have a long-term strategy. I do, and you don't."

"That's why I won the first 11 games before you won a game," he said. "Now even telling you that, let me give you a warning. It's not easy to train yourself to be a long term thinker. I'll show you what I mean. Let's play a few more games."

We played for four more hours. We played over 40 games of checkers during those four hours. Some were quick. Some were longer and more difficult. Out of that whole series of consecutive games I won three. That's all. I was frustrated. I thought surely I was smart enough to play checkers. But out of over 50 total games that night I won four.

After we finished playing it was now 1:30 in the morning.

Dexter said, "Let's take a break. We went into the kitchen and drank cold bottles of water and ate oatmeal raisin cookies. Dexter pulled some licorice from a cabinet and chewed on that for a few minutes and then sat down at the kitchen table and I joined him.

Dexter said, "Ron we played a lot of games and you didn't do so hot, did you?"

I answered, "Dexter I didn't do so hot at all."

He said, "Don't worry. No sweat. You're going to get better. But listen, the difference is not who's a better checker player. The difference is who's a better thinker. It doesn't mean that I'm smarter than you, or you're smarter than me. I've learned to think in a certain way. I've learned to think long term. I've trained myself to think many moves ahead. When I say many moves ahead, I do not mean just in a game like this. I mean in life itself."

Dexter and I played checkers for our next several visits. I knew he was trying to teach me strategy and long term thinking. We didn't just play that night, but we played for several months when I would return for different nights with Dexter.

Some months later, when we were sitting up late one night, playing our hundredth game of checkers on that visit Dexter said, "You need to read something."

He brought out a magazine article from a major well known business publication. This article said that the trend in major corporate training was to use board games like checkers to determine who among the executives of a particular company were the best strategic thinkers. It stated that board games revealed the way a person's mind grasped and solved a problem.

I said, "Dexter, did you decide to teach me through the game of checkers because you read this article and you knew that board games like checkers had become part of corporate executive training?"

He laughed and said, "No Ron. I just found the article this week and I just wanted you to see it because it backs up what I've been telling you. It's a confirmation of what I've been teaching you."

For the next few months Dexter focused on my mind. He knew that I had a research background; that I love to read; that I go through hundreds of books every year looking for information and insight to help people and to serve God. Dexter knew that I'd had a number of years of formal education with a master's degree and had worked in a doctoral program in a large southern university.

Dexter also recognized the fact that with all that knowledge and formal education I still was too limited in my ability to think things through. On that first night when we played checkers until the early morning hours, Dexter had emphasized to me his perception that I used my emotions far too much in making decisions.

Dexter said, "I have watched you. As I've watched you I know that you get very excited and you become emotionally involved in a situation or in a person or in a decision. I want to teach you how to step back from a situation and not be so emotionally involved in it. I want you to back away and be able to look at the situation with careful logic."

He said, "I did not do this naturally. I had to learn to do it. I learned to do it because I'm an emotional guy too. I really care about people and I feel for what they're going through. But I realized many years ago, that I could not successfully help other people unless I could use independent judgment. I couldn't help them unless I could make good clear-headed decisions. If I could not do that I might end up supporting someone in a decision that they wanted to come true, that they thought they needed and hoped for, but it actually might not have been the best thing for them. So if I was going to be an educator and mentor and a guide to other people and I was going to be able to help them, I had to learn to back away and to see situations much more clearly."

By this time it was five o'clock in the morning. We went back and played another hour of checkers until six o'clock.

Then Dexter looked over the checkerboard and said, "Do you want another round, or do you want to stretch and walk around?"

At that point I was all for stretching and walking around. We stood up and went outside. There was just a tinge of light to the horizon and the slightest touch of a cool breeze stirring the water. It was almost 6:30 by now as we walked around the edge of the shoreline.

Dexter said, "I know we didn't get to any of your questions on this visit. I hope that's OK. If you have any questions that are really important that you need an answer to then why don't we take a few minutes and look at those."

I said, "Dexter you have been led by God on this visit because I needed what you said."

Dexter smiled and said, "You know the truth is I felt in my heart that you needed this lesson when I prayed about your visit. I knew that I had been teaching you a great deal about a lot of stuff. I thought you needed to know how to think. You needed to be trained to know how to get into the middle something and understand how to help people without your emotions clouding your understanding."

He said, "I actually prayed that you would be open to me teaching you this today."

I was emotional for a moment and overcome with gratitude that Dexter loved me and God loved me so much that God would guide Dexter to help me become a better thinker.

I took Dexter by the arm and said, "Dex, I cannot thank you enough. This has been one of our greatest nights together. When you started with the statement that people are basically stupid, in all honesty, I did not know what you meant. I tried to say that I did, but I was confused. Now I see what you mean. People don't know how to think. They choose to see things the way they want them to be, not the way they really are."

Dex said, "You got it. That's exactly what I wanted you to see."

Some years later I was reading a book co-authored by a man named Bob Waterman. Waterman had co-written an eariler book with Tom Peters in the middle eighties called *In Search of Excellence*. My paraphrase of what Bob Waterman wrote in the new book is that, "The greatest struggle that people have when they try to create personal and business success is they fight reality. They don't become friends with facts. They insist on seeing life the way they want it to be, not the way it really is. They fight and kick and struggle when they should have been using all that energy to embrace reality and build something on that understanding.

This was what Dexter wanted me to see. So many people waste time in the attempt to convince themselves of something that is not really true. They don't become, as Bob Waterman said, "friends with facts."

Dexter is a realist. He was then; he is now. Dexter, always deals with the way it is, not the way he wants it to be. Because of that, he is able to develop a practical solution for situations. His solutions are based in reality, not in fantasy.

One of the greatest lessons Dexter ever taught me was to become friends with facts and to think clearly, logically, and not emotionally. He taught me the importance of making decisions based on principles and not my personal preferences.

When the sun fully came up that morning I was full of appreciation. All I could do was thank Dexter again for what he had labored to teach me that night. It was a beautiful morning with a mist off the water. The fishermen were coming and going; some finishing the night; some going out for the morning. Activity on the lake was beginning to stir.

Dexter said, "You know Ron, I'm going to do things a bit different. Let's have some breakfast."

We went to Denny's and had breakfast. We returned to the lake house at 8:30. By nine o'clock Dexter had already gone to bed, and I was sitting on the edge of the bed in the guest room.

I remember praying, "Lord, this has been so important for me. I don't think I even fully realize what you have taught me through Dexter this time, but I'm grateful."

With that sense of thankfulness I drifted off to sleep. My alarm was meaningless. I overslept by two hours. I got home later than I had planned, but I knew it was worth it. When I explained to Amy what Dexter had taught me on this visit she knew it was worth it as well.

That was my latest dawn with Dexter.

CHAPTER II

Why God Matters

As I have described my mentoring adventure with Dexter, it's possible that you have wondered at times about the source and development of Dexter's spiritual life. He frequently mentioned God and he often quoted the Bible. He still does. I was with Dexter recently, and he was eager to spend time in prayer and seeking God. He was like that in all those early years together as well.

My own Christian background influenced my spiritual receptivity to Dexter. When I was growing up in South Eastern Kentucky, my mother and father never went to church. I had no spiritual training, except for an occasional visit to Sunday School, and an occasional trip to vacation Bible school in the summer. My mom and dad were morally upright people, but had no relationship with Jesus Christ while I was growing up.

I'm an only child and Sunday morning was a family time for the three of us. My mother, who grew up on a farm, would cook a big country breakfast on Sunday morning. She'd cook gravy, biscuits, pork chops, fried potatoes, fried apples, and occasionally even fried chicken. We would eat until there was no room left and my dad and I would read the newspaper together. I would read the comics and he would read the rest. Mom would clean up after breakfast and church time would come and go with us sitting around and just being together. Sunday was a day like any other, except there was no school and no work.

My first acquaintance with spiritual life came when I visited a Southern Baptist Sunday School. The teacher visited my home one week and asked if any one in our family knew Christ personally. My parents were uncomfortable, and I was confused. The teacher was loving and gentle and sincere, but none of us came to a full understanding of what he was trying to say. It wasn't his fault. He tried very hard. I'm grateful for his efforts to this day.

The change occurred for me when a new pastor moved to our small community. He was Paul Stoneking, the newly appointed pastor of the first United Methodist Church. He was a sensation. No one like him had ever come to town before. He was a dramatic and exceptional preacher who soon had the church packed to hear his sermons. He would conduct meetings on the street and in the jail. The whole town was astir with this unusually effective Christian leader.

After a few months of hearing stories of his ministry, I asked my dad if he would take me to hear him one Sunday morning. I was 13 years old. My dad was curious and agreed to take me.

We went to the service and it was so full that we could only find seats on the second row from the front. I sat with my dad and heard a dramatic presentation of the truth about Jesus Christ. The pastor spoke of Jesus' life and death and resurrection. He spoke as if Jesus were alive today, and he said that anyone could know him, and that Jesus wanted to know us in relationship as well.

It was as if I were isolated in the service. After several minutes, I felt as if I were the only one there. I felt that everything the man was saying was aimed squarely at me. He then asked that those who wanted to ask Jesus Christ to come into their life to walk to the front and kneel down at an altar rail.

I was scared. I wanted to go forward, but I couldn't move. The conflict only increased as he led the congregation in a song of invitation. I did not know the song at the time. I do now. It goes like this: "Softly and tenderly Jesus is calling, calling oh sinner come home." The chorus is "Come home. Come home. You who are weary come home."

I was only 13, but I suddenly felt that the song was meant for me. I felt that I needed to come home to God. I looked down and saw that I was clutching the back of the wooden seat with such force that my knuckles had turned white.

When we reached the last verse of the song, and the service had almost concluded, I suddenly found myself at the front. To this day I do not recall how it happened, or what occurred. It's very simple, I must have stepped out and walked forward. I was kneeling at the front with almost a dozen other people who had come forward.

The pastor made his way down this row of kneeling individuals until he arrived at me. He asked me why I'd come. I mumbled something about wanting what he talked about. He led me in a prayer and encouraged me to ask Jesus Christ into my life. I followed his prayer and prayed it with sincerity. No thunder rolled and no lightning flashed. I felt no great ripple of emotion. It was all quiet and almost emotionally empty. But I prayed the prayer and I knew that I meant the prayer when I asked Jesus Christ to come into my life and change me and be my personal Lord and Savior.

I did not know it at the time, but my father had come forward as well. He was kneeling at the other end of the altar. The people who were helping the pastor counsel that morning thought that my dad had come to support me. So no one spoke with him. No one prayed with him. No one helped him. My dad did not come into a full relationship with Christ for two more years, but that morning at least was the beginning of his desire for that relationship.

I went home and my mother who had made the big country breakfast was waiting for me. My mother and I had always been extremely close. She'd been my greatest supporter, and my best friend for all the years of my childhood and youth. My mother had always supported me in everything.

So imagine my shock and amazement when I walked into the kitchen and said, "Mom the greatest thing just happened to me. I asked Jesus Christ to come into my life."

My mother turned on me with a viciousness I had never before encountered. She said, "Don't ever say the name of Jesus in this house again. If you do, you can leave."

I walked to my bedroom stunned. This was my mother, who had always been the best friend I'd had in the world. She had supported me in everything. She had loved me through every situation. Now she was telling me to leave home if I wanted Jesus in my life?

I was shocked. I knelt beside my bed and the tears exploded. I wept for 20 minutes, not knowing what to say. I looked up and said a prayer, "Oh God I believe what I did today, and I believe in Jesus and I'm not turning back."

I went on a school trip that week. While I was away my mother, who had been overcome by what had happened to me, went to visit that same pastor. She knocked on his door and with tears said, "My son prayed with you Sunday, and I need to pray with you as well. Would you help me?"

That pastor led my mother to Jesus Christ. A week later my mother and I were baptized together. Then, as I said, my father came to Christ two years later.

I immediately developed an intense hunger to know the Bible. I would study my Bible for 1 to 2 hours a day after school. I began to hunger for more personal knowledge of God. When I was 15 I began to sense that God was calling me to public ministry. I began to spend time everyday after school in our local church to pray and seek God's direction. God became very real. His presence was amazingly powerful. During those few years I grew in depth and knowledge after I finished high school and went to college and developed further.

God began to open opportunities for me to speak in different churches and organizations. I met my wife Amy and went on to seminary and graduate school. For all these years, the constant center of my life has been Jesus Christ. His reality, His power, His presence, His guidance all have remained at the core of who I am.

When I met Dexter Yager I was already committed to know Christ and follow Him and obey Him. I had already pastored three churches and had worked with the great Dr. Charles Stanley in Atlanta. I had already spent nearly seven years of my life conducting crusades that were like small Billy Graham meetings with multiple numbers of churches supporting the event.

When Dexter would speak to me about Jesus Christ or ask me to pray or discuss the Bible with me I was always eager to do so. Dexter, I knew, had a living relationship with Christ. I knew that obedience to God was his greatest priority.

He had explained to me on one occasion, how early in his business growth he was involved in a weekend training conference. He called it a family reunion. The family in this case, consisted of the people professionally connected to him in his business organization. He said that because the meeting went late Saturday night there were large numbers of people who were unable to leave in time to be at their local churches on Sunday.

So he had an idea. Dexter decided with Birdie's full support, that he would have an interdenominational, non-sectarian, Christian worship service that would be available to whomever wanted to attend. It would not be a part of the official weekend. No one had to come, but it would be available for those who wanted to be a part of it.

Dexter said that he never realized the firestorm of criticism and opposition that would erupt over that simple decision to help people have a place to go to church and worship when they did not have time to get home for the weekend. He intended it, he explained, as a way to give those who wanted it a worship opportunity. The criticism occurred when certain people began to accuse him of mixing business and religion. But he always reminded those critics, that no one had to come to the service and it was entirely voluntary. People came because they wanted to come. He was merely making it available.

Over the years Dexter has made available, similar Sunday mornings around the world. Hundreds of thousands, possibly millions of people have attended the services. I have personally had the great privilege to speak in a number of these Sunday mornings over the last 20 years. We have seen tens of thousands of people every year make first-time adult commitments to Christ. It has been one of the great avenues of effective evangelism in this generation.

There's no way to measure what happens in these services. I have spoken at meetings where five to 10,000 people have walked forward to make sincere commitments to Jesus Christ. Dexter has been committed through the years to follow up at these meetings. He has made available at his own expense, tapes, books, Bibles, and now CDs to give people spiritual support and training. He has encouraged people to become a part of local evangelical churches. This is one of the great ministries in America.

I was with a Southern Baptist pastor in Texas on one occasion when we had just finished a great Yager Christian worship service in Fort Worth. This pastor leaned over to me and said, "You know, this is the greatest evangelism I've ever seen anywhere in the world!" He said this because people were coming to Christ by the thousands.

This still happens to this day. There are Sunday morning services sponsored by Dexter Yager that take place in every part of the globe.

There are thousands every month who hear a clear, simple presentation of Jesus Christ every week. People will come to Christ in commitment and surrender as a result of these services.

I knew early that Dexter had a Christian commitment that was world shaping. His influence for business and success was immense. But his influence for God was even bigger. It is to this day.

I was speaking one Sunday morning at a Yager Free Enterprise Celebration. There were over 15,000 people in the Sunday morning service who had come voluntarily on their own because they wanted a spiritual dimension to life. I noticed that there was an unusual reaction in the crowd as I was speaking. I was midway through the message when I realized that the audience—all 15,000 of them—were reacting to something that I could not see. I turned around and Dexter Yager had walked onto the stage and was standing behind me.

Dexter usually did not attend that part of the service because he'd usually been up until seven or eight in the morning counseling people and praying with them. So he or Birdie would slip in late, or sometimes slip out of the service entirely because they were so tired.

This particular day I was surprised to see him standing behind me midway through the sermon. Dexter walked up and put his arm on my shoulder and asked for the microphone.

After I handed it to Him, he looked at the crowd and said, "I want you to support and believe everything Ron is saying. Because when he tells you to ask Jesus Christ in your life, he's telling you to do what I've already done."

He said, "One night I went into a Methodist church as a young man. It was empty and dark. I walked into the sanctuary and made my way to the platform where the pulpit stood. I turned on one light and walked upon the platform and stood behind the pulpit for a few minutes."

The crowd was totally quiet as Dexter told his story.

Then Dexter said, "I knelt down beside that pulpit and I asked Jesus Christ to be real in my life and to live within me and to use my life for His glory anyway He chose; wherever He chose; with whomever He chose; in whatever way He chose. I had come to a relationship with Christ at 6 years of age and I was now deepening that earlier commitment."

He continued, "I made a surrender and a commitment that God used to totally changed my life and direction."

To every one's surprise, Dexter suddenly knelt down on the platform with me. Seeing what was happening, I knelt beside him.

Dexter said, "This is what I did that day. I humbled myself before God. This is what I want to encourage all of you, thousands of you, to do today. Ask Jesus Christ in your life as well."

This crowd had only known Dexter as an outstanding business leader. They had listened to him speak during the weekend as an exceptional business and success communicator. They were now seeing Dexter Yager in an entirely different way. He was a simple man who humbled himself before God.

At that point I abandoned any thought of continuing the sermon as Dexter and I stood. I took the microphone, looked at the crowd and said, "Do you want Jesus Christ to live in your life? Why don't you come to the front now to make a public acknowledgment of your surrender to Jesus Christ."

People came by the thousands. It was a moment of rare spiritual power.

That's the kind of man Dexter Yager is. He's not arrogant. He's not uppity. He's not demanding. He is a genuine Christian. His wife Birdie shares with him a wonderful relationship with Christ.

Birdie Yager has a heart for God so big that she is always seeking bigger experiences with the Lord she loves. Birdie is just as committed to Christ and just as committed to knowing the Bible as is Dexter. Dexter has tremendous respect for the quality of her life with Christ. They're a great team.

I remember a number of years ago late one night when I received a phone message from a good friend. He told me that Dexter had nearly died in the night. He'd had a devastating stroke and was in the hospital. I was on the phone for most of the evening trying to locate someone in the hospital with whom I could talk. I finally connected with Birdie who told me that yes, Dexter was in grave danger.

This was just a short time after I had first started working with Dexter. I'd only been going through my mentoring adventure with him for 2 or 3 years. Now I thought I was going to lose him and I would not have the benefit of his training and his wisdom any longer.

I joined with thousands of others around the world to pray for Dexter's recovery.

Thankfully he did recover. He had two other major strokes and a number of other cardiac incidents. As a result of those experiences Dexter became even more committed to good health. He changed his diet and his lifestyle. He lost a great amount of weight. He developed a commitment to bodybuilding and physical training. He is in excellent condition today. His commitment to healthy living has paid off abundantly.

But I know the truth. I know why Dexter lived. I know why he didn't die in the hospital when even his wife Birdie didn't know if he would survive. I know what really happened.

God intervened. God spared him. God answered prayer, because God was not finished with Dexter.

I went on a trip with Amy and Birdie and Dexter to Europe a short time after Dexter was released from the hospital. He still had some difficulty in using the right side of his body. His arm was weak and he walked with a slight limp. I spent a week watching Dexter pour his heart out to people even though he had just nearly died weeks before. I watched him pray for people. I watched him help individuals. I watched him as he gave and gave and gave without any thought for his own personal welfare. I was there when he ministered to people and trained them during a difficult international trip when he himself was not physically what he had been the previous year. I will never forget his giving spirit through that difficult time.

As I said earlier, Dexter has made extraordinary progress physically. He is in excellent physical condition at this point in his life. As he nears his seventies he is in better condition than many men are in their forties. That's the result of commitment on his part. He always said "Success is a decision." In Dexter's case, you would have to say that fitness is also a decision.

But beyond all that is Dexter's continuing sense of God's calling. Dexter feels a sense of destiny. He's not perfect. Who is? He never claims to be. Dexter has a heart for God that never waivers.

All the times when I'm with him when we sit up in the early morning hours and wait for the dawn, part of our time is always spent in prayer. Part of it is always spent seeking God.

I was with Dexter just recently visiting him at his home in

Florida. At three o'clock in the morning when we finished a detailed discussion related to his business, Dexter did what he always does.

He said, "Ron let's pray. Dexter opened his soul and asked God to help the people whom Dexter was involved with. He prayed for me, as he always does. He prayed for Amy and Allison, our daughter, and Jonathan, our son.

When Jonathan was born Birdie told me that God had a special plan for him. We'd already known that about Allison. She's had a special calling of God in her life for a number of years. Dexter and Birdie's spiritual role in Jonathan's life is significant.

Amy and I wanted to have another child and had for a number of years been unable to do so. We had enjoyed our daughter and as she was approaching her teen years we so especially wanted another child. One day Amy told me with excitement that she was pregnant. We thanked God and told Dexter and Birdie. They rejoiced with us. But four months into the pregnancy Amy miscarried and we lost the child.

Sometime after that Dexter said, "Ron, let me help you arrange an adoption."

I'd never considered this before. I'd already thought that maybe because of our ages it might be our last opportunity. Dexter helped arrange an adoption of a little boy.

The week of the adoption there were some challenges and unexpected situations. We had the nursery prepared, my wife was eager for the baby, and we had purchased plane tickets to bring him home. But suddenly it didn't work out. We didn't get the baby. It didn't happen.

Amy and I remember calling Dexter and Birdie at four o'clock in the morning and crying with them on the phone. We thought this was our last opportunity.

But on that November night Dexter said, "No. Birdie and I are going to pray that God will do a miracle for you. We are going to pray that God will do something so amazing that you will know it's from Him."

In February, just months later, Amy became pregnant again. Nine months after that she gave birth to Jonathan Dexter Lee Ball. The name Jonathan is based on the Jonathan of the Bible. Dexter is from Dexter Yager. The name Lee is after my father because his middle name is Lee and so is mine. And of course, Ball is our family name.

Jonathan is now 10 years old and Birdie and Dexter always check on him and remind me that God has a plan for him.

They also love Allison and they believe that God has a plan for her as well. In fact Dexter trained Allison personally in business development.

When Allison was eight years old Dexter said, "Take her off all allowances."

She was not happy about that.

But Dexter said, "Your daughter is special and God's going to use her. I want you to train her to earn her own money."

Allison developed a pencil business a year later that she called Positive Pencils International. For years she has sold positive pencils personally developed by her all over the world. She has been careful with her money and has done well financially. She is taking care of her own education because she has earned her own money. Allison will tell you today that she owes Dexter a debt of tremendous gratitude.

Dexter has always had a spiritual interest in both of our children. When Jonathan was born, the son we thought we might never have, Dexter said, "God is in this. This is an answer to prayer. You have Allison," whom he personally had trained financially for years and had taken great personal interests in, "and now you have Jonathan," whom Dexter and Birdie had actually prayed for, "who was a miraculous answer to prayer himself."

Dexter has been a vital part of my family. Not just in mentoring for me personally, but in the development of my children and the enrichment of my marriage. Amy has great confidence in Dexter. She always encourages him to tell me what I need and to stretch me where I need to stretch. She has great confidence in Birdie, because she knows that their hearts are honest. She knows that they have one motivation, and that is to help people all over the world.

It's obvious why I love this man and his wife. It's apparent why he means so much to me personally. His influence on my thinking, on my view of success, on my spiritual development, and on my professional development has been beyond calculation. I know that Dexter still prays for me and still prays for all the people he loves everywhere. He has always been a consistent mentor and a consistent guide. I am grateful that God led me to Dexter Yager on that first dawn years ago. I am grateful that my wife has benefited from all the training that Dexter freely gave me. I am grateful that I have been privileged to see tens of thousands of people come to know Christ through the opportunity Dexter has given me to speak at his great conventions and at many Sunday morning services.

It's amazing. I now have spoken live to over 6 million people throughout the world. I've seen millions of my tapes and CDs circulate in different countries. I have written books with Dexter, that have sold over a million copies and each book has contained a message of Jesus Christ.

How could I have ever imagined that all that would happen when I first visited Dexter's lake house and he gave me a phone number and said call me and come and visit me? How could I ever imagine what would happen in my life because I was willing to sit up and have a dawn with Dexter, and then a second and third and a fourth? Now there have been so many I have lost count.

I still have dawns with Dexter. I had one last month. I'm already scheduled for another one in the coming months, because I can't get enough! It's been years and I still can't get enough because I want to be like Dexter as I get older. I want to be always growing; always hungry; always developing; always growing in my desire and knowledge for more of God and more of success for God's glory.

When I first met Dexter, I wasn't sure whether success and Christians mixed. A short time before we met, my friend Charles Stanley had lunch with me. He said something that had a tremendous influence on my thinking.

He said, "Ron, too many Christians are filled with poverty thinking. They're more focused on their limitations than on God's possibilities."

He said, "You want to do something great for God and God wants to do something great through you. You need to let Him."

When Dr. Stanley told me that I had no idea that God had already prepared Dexter Yager to take me to the next level.

When I met Dexter, I realized that it was possible to be immensely successful, financially and professionally to do it all for the greater glory to the God who called you. I realized that it was possible to be committed to Christ and also have personal and financial success. I knew that God wanted to use people in ways I never realized before.

My dawns with Dexter have been a part of my life now for 20 years. I hope they'll be a part of my life from now on because every dawn with Dexter has always brought a great new day!

EPILOGUE .

As you've journeyed with me through the mentoring experiences that I've had with Dexter Yager, have there been moments when you have hungered for more in your life? Have you wanted a deeper understanding of God's purpose and plan for you personally?

I want to encourage you, as I know Dexter would, to do certain things right now. One is very simple and basic. Open your life to Jesus Christ. Allow Him to be your Savior. Recognize that he died for you on the cross, rose from the dead, and is alive today. Jesus said in John 17:3 "This is life that you may know Me and the Father who sent me."

The most quoted verse in the Bible is John 3:16: "For God so loved the world that He gave His only begotten son. That whoever believes in Him should not perish but have everlasting life."

The word believe is the operative word. In the original Greek language it means to believe in Jesus so much that you're willing to throw the whole weight of your whole life on Him. You're willing to depend on Him alone. Not to depend on your religion, and not your efforts to be good, and not your involvement in your church, and not religious ceremony or ritual, but Jesus Christ alone.

The Bible says in Galatians 2:16 "That by works of religion no one is made right with God." I want to encourage you, as I know Dexter would, to make certain of your living relationship with Jesus Christ. Jesus is God come in human flesh to reach you; to change you; to be your Savior; to do for you which you can never do for yourself.

The Bible teaches in the book of Romans "That all have sinned and come short of the glory of God." That means you cannot save yourself. You cannot do it through your being a good church person.

You can only experience salvation through a Savior, and that Savior is Jesus Christ.

I also want to encourage you to make a commitment to some hard choices. Those hard choices involve disciplining your life. Discipline not only in terms of spiritual growth, Bible study and prayer, but in terms of your own efforts to give God your life as an example of commitment.

Remember what Dexter said on one occasion? Christians ought to out think and out work and out love everyone else. Why don't you decide to do that right now? Don't be socialistic. Earn your way. Prove yourself. Show your commitment.

I learned from Dexter the necessity to develop mental and physical toughness. That's what you need as well. You need to stop complaining and whining. Stop moaning over life's unfairness and determine that you're going to be a warrior. You're going to be a successful soldier. You're going to be someone who is going to reach for the high goals in life.

Don't be afraid of money. It's true the Bible says that a love of money is a root of all kinds of evil. But notice the Bible does not say that money is the root of evil but that an unbalanced inappropriate love of money is a root of all kinds of evil. Money itself is not wrong. It depends on what you want to do with it.

Deuteronomy 8:18 says that it is God who gives you power to get wealth. Proverbs 3:5,6 speaks of trusting the Lord with all your heart and leaning not to your own understanding and in all your ways acknowledging him and he will direct your paths. Right after those verses it says that God will bless you with abundance and your barns will overflow.

God's not against success or prosperity or money. He's only against those things when you compromise morally or spiritually to get them. Learn an example from Dexter Yager. Honest effort and honest achievement are good. The Bible says "Whatever you do, do to the glory of God." So why don't you decide to give God your best effort and your best commitment?

I've learned so many things from Dexter at all these dawns over the years. I've learned about delayed gratification, hard work, positive attitude, love for people, and putting God first. I've learned so many lessons that still resonate in my life to this day.